Rob White
SERIES EDITOR

Colin MacCabe and David Meeker
SERIES CONSULTANTS

Cinema is a fragile medium. Many of the great classic films of the past now exist, if at all, in damaged or incomplete prints. Concerned about the deterioration in the physical state of our film heritage, the National Film and Television Archive, a Division of the British Film Institute, has compiled a list of 360 key films in the history of the cinema. The long-term goal of the Archive is to build a collection of perfect showprints of these films, which will then be screened regularly at the Museum of the Moving Image in London in a year-round repertory.

BFI Film Classics is a series of books commissioned to stand alongside these titles. Authors, including film critics and scholars, film-makers, novelists, historians and those distinguished in the arts, have been invited to write on a film of their choice, drawn from the Archive's list. Each volume presents the author's own insights into the chosen film, together with a brief production history and detailed credits, notes and bibliography. The numerous illustrations have been specially made from the Archive's own prints.

With new titles published each year, the BFI Film Classics series is a unique, authoritative and highly readable guide to the great films of world cinema.

Could scarcely be improved upon ... informative, intelligent, jargon-free companions.
The Observer

Cannily but elegantly packaged BFI Classics will make for a neat addition to the most discerning shelves.
New Statesman & Society

D1583864

James Fox and Donald Cammell during the shoot

BFI FILM CLASSICS

PERFORMANCE

. . . .

Colin MacCabe

 Publishing

First published in 1998 by the
BRITISH FILM INSTITUTE
21 Stephen Street, London W1P 2LN

Copyright © Colin MacCabe 1998

Reprinted 2002

The British Film Institute
is the UK national agency with
responsibility for encouraging the arts
of film and television and
conserving them in the national interest.

British Library Cataloguing-in-Publication Data
A catalogue record for this book is available from the British Library

ISBN 0–85170–670–3

Series design by
Andrew Barron & Collis Clements Associates

Typesetting by
D R Bungay Associates, Burghfield, Berks.

Printed in Great Britain by The Cromwell Press, Wiltshire

CONTENTS

. . . .

For Flavia with whom I first saw *Performance*

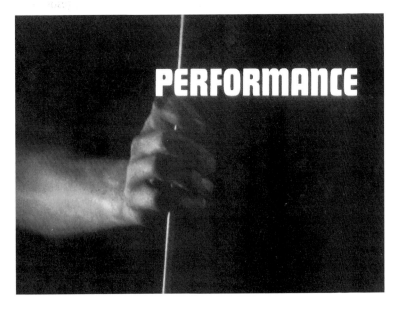

The opening title

ACKNOWLEDGMENTS

. . . .

I would like to thank Jonathon Green for providing not only much of the bibliography but also most of the books. Nick Groom, Duncan Petrie, Harriet Vyner, Jon Savage and Ric Senat also provided crucial secondary material. Kevin Macdonald generously shared the fruits of the research for the film that he and Chris Rodley made on Donald Cammell. Mick Eaton told me how to write the book. Ed Buscombe and David Meeker encouraged me to undertake the project.

One of the great pleasures of writing the book was to meet so many of those who were involved in making the film. Sandy Lieberson provided not only his memories but also the contents of his attic. David Cammell, Deborah Dixon and Frank Mazzola were generous both with their time and the papers and letters in their possession. Christopher Gibbs, James Fox, Mick Jagger, Annabel Steele, Stanley Meadows, Jack Nitszche, Dick Polak, Nic Roeg and Johnny Shannon were extraordinarily helpful in their interviews. Tony Elliott filled in the details of the British release.

Damian M, Johnny Shannon, Nick Groom, Sandy Lieberson, James Fox, Nic Roeg, Tamara Horowitz, David Cammell, Kevin Macdonald and Paula Jalfon all read the text and made suggestions for detailed corrections and amendments. My editor Rob White and my research assistant Elayne Tobin improved the text considerably with their suggested revisions.

INTRODUCTION

. . . .

I doubt if I have ever been so affected by any film as I was by my first viewing of *Performance*. I went to see it the weekend it opened in London in January 1971. The pre-publicity was extraordinary. I hadn't read the Richard Schickel review in *Time* which called it 'the most disgusting, the most completely worthless film I have seen since I began reviewing'[1] nor John Simon's *New York Times* piece that named it 'this indescribably sleazy self-indulgent and meretricious film'.[2] But I did know that Warner Bros. had sat on the film for years terrified of the immorality they had perpetrated and there were rumours that the experience had so scarred James Fox that he had abandoned the most successful acting career of the decade.

Indeed, as the lights went down I had that feeling of scared excitement which accompanies the onset of a new sexual desire or a strange hallucinogenic drug. Nor was I to be disappointed. As the finest British gangster film ever made metamorphosed into a psycho-sexual drama by Bataille out of Artaud, the film delivered an anatomy of masculinity which promised a genuine liberation from the cage of gender. In the astonishing final moments of the film, as Chas shoots an acquiescent Turner and the film breaks every rule of spatial construction; as we enter Turner's head and exit through the roof of 81 Powis Square; and as the drones and pulses of the synthesizer which have accompanied us through the movie reach a triumphant climax, the movie delivered a genuine sense of release, a taste of freedom.

A quarter of a century on, the film retains much of its extraordinary power. It is, defiantly, of its time but it is not dated. The power comes from the precise and accurate recording of two different worlds. The film takes us on a tour of the bars and the clubs of the gangsters of working-class London. The trial in early 1969 of the Kray twins made clear that there was a whole world of crime and corruption in London which had evaded any representation, be it fact or fiction. *Performance*, shot before the trial, simply inhabited this world, sketching its habits and dialects for a generation of cop shows to imitate.

But, *Performance*, in that effortless productivity which is the mark of a true classic, is not satisfied with having delivered one new world to the viewer. In the second half of the film, as we leave the streets of London to sequester ourselves in Powis Square, we enter the isolated world of the fading rock star. If Hollywood had provided the first archetype of the media recluse with the real Howard Hughes or the fictional Norma Desmond, it was rock music with its necessary corollaries of sex and drugs which provided the definitive version. *Performance* was onto this very early, taking Brian Jones of the Rolling Stones as its model. It is his house at 1 Courtfield Road which inspired Turner's, it is his girlfriend, Anita Pallenberg (in her only major film role), who is the principal commentator on the action and it was the man who designed Jones' house, Christopher Gibbs, who was the designer on the film.

And Gibbs indeed is one of the keys to the film. In an early draft of the script Donald Cammell describes Turner's bedroom as 'decorated predominantly in the Gibbsan Moroccan manner' and the adjective makes clear how distinctive Gibbs had become as an interior designer. Gibbs was also a key figure in the Chelsea set that Peter Wollen in his excellent article analysed as central to the genesis of *Performance*.[3] This group of young decadent aristocrats who received their media baptism in the late 50s provided in the 60s the link between the worlds of pop and crime. It is the privilege of the upper classes to collect what is in fashion, be it objects or people, and in the 60s nothing was more fashionable than pop music and crime.

Much of this is traditional – crime has been glamorised and entertainers have provided sex for the upper classes throughout English history; indeed these phenomena if not as old as the hills are certainly as old as cities themselves. Dick Turpin and Nell Gwynne are only two of the most famous examples. What was new was the sex. Not sex itself – for the theatre had always provided pretty girls and epicene boys – but the rough trade offered by the genuinely criminal. Of course it is difficult to know how new this really was. Harry Flowers' grandfather may well have been one of the rent boys forced to testify against Oscar Wilde. Be that as it may, it was not until the 60s that the rigid class divide between aristocrat decadent and proletarian criminal was defiantly breached under the sign of gay sex. So it was that the Chelsea set, of which Donald Cammell was a member, provided a meeting place for the two most astonishing sources of energy and mobility in 60s London.

However, *Performance* is anything but the attempt to produce a vérité account of London in the 60s. If the film is astonishing for the accuracy of its representations, those representations themselves are merely the elements from which the film weaves its magic as it seeks to imagine the impossible and Utopian dream of a fusion between its two worlds. It is that fusion which the film performs and which produces an ending that Jon Savage has aptly described as 'satisfying and curiously hopeful'.[4]

THE BACK STORY

. . . .

Like almost all films, *Performance*'s history stretches back long before its production in 1968 or its release more than two years later. But there is no doubt that it all begins, as it was to end, with the extraordinary figure of Donald Cammell. Rumour makes Cammell's godfather Aleister Crowley, the most notorious magician of the twentieth century, and it is not altogether fanciful to see a kind of occult curse following Cammell through an extraordinarily gifted and full life which was, in conventional terms, dogged by failure after failure. But the failures were to come after *Performance*. The film itself must have seemed at the time like simply a moment on a rising graph of almost effortless success.

He was born in Edinburgh on 17 January 1934 the son of Charles Richard Cammell (the name is a Gaelic alternate spelling of Campbell) and his second wife Iona Macdonald. Donald's father had inherited an enormous fortune from the shipbuilding firm of Cammell Laird and had used it to develop his talents as a writer and aesthete. In the 20s with his first wife he had bought and renovated a huge château in Burgundy but the marriage ended when the crash wiped out his fortune. Back in Scotland he married in 1932 a beautiful Highland girl Iona Macdonald and they lived in the Outlook Tower which had in its roof a camera obscura from which the whole of Edinburgh could be seen.

Donald was a precocious child who by the age of three was drawing and painting and was doted on by both his parents. His father was now earning a living as an editor and writer and had become a foremost exponent of Scottish nationalism, regularly commissioned by the *Scotsman* to write odes on notable events. It gives something of the flavour of this unreconstructed Romantic that he combined his artistic pursuits with a keen interest in fencing at which he became Scottish champion. The family, to which a brother David was added in 1937, was soon to be disrupted by the war. One of the first results of the forced transitions of those times was the family's encounter with Aleister Crowley. The notorious magician and poet was living in a house in Devon close to where the Cammells had moved to escape the bombing and Cammell *père* became such friends with Crowley and so convinced of his importance as a writer and a thinker that he became Crowley's biographer. Cammell's book had hardly issued from the presses than another and less flattering biography, entitled *The Great Beast*, ensured that the image of Crowley that was to pass into common currency was that of a sick and perverted monomaniac. But the family remained on friendly terms. Crowley was to cast David's horoscope and if the story that Crowley was Donald's godfather defies both chronology and logic, there is enough of a connection to have rendered it plausible down the years.

The next move for the Cammell brothers was to the Highlands of Scotland where David stayed with his grandmother and Donald went to a prep school in Fort Augustus. This is the only period of Donald's childhood which appears anything other than conventionally happy. He was pathologically homesick, so distraught that his mother came and took him away in the winter of 1942–3 and back to London where he was soon happily ensconced in Shrewsbury House School near Thames Ditton. His precocious drawing ability was such that his father had his work exhibited at the Royal Drawing Society from the age of eight onwards and his artistic abilities were complemented by the attributes of a good sportsman, in particular he excelled at both cricket and football. From Shrewsbury House he progressed to Westminster and from there he went to Byam Shaw and won a scholarship to the Royal Academy. His apprenticeship as a painter was completed when he went in the early 50s to study with Annigoni in Florence. Annigoni was then the leading portrait painter in Europe and a friend of Donald's father who had written a book about him. Donald returned to London and set up as a portrait painter with a studio in Chelsea at Flood Street. He was immediately successful and in 1953 his portrait of the Marquis of Dufferin and Ava dressed as a pageboy for the Coronation was judged the society portrait of the year.

It wasn't just for painting that Cammell showed a precocious talent. Sex was, from the earliest tussles with girl cousins, a Cammell trademark and the studio at Flood Street was as famous for its beddings as for its sittings. There is many a respectable society matron who might blush to recount to her granddaughter her deeds at the Flood Street studio. Almost all the gossip, and there is much gossip about Cammell, is of heterosexual sex but the world in which he moved, and of which his studio was one of the focal points, was one where homosexuality was open and unremarkable. Nik Cohn describes the ambience well:

> At first the game was distinctly upper class, made up of a few
> discontented debs ... and a gaggle of public schoolboys, in search
> of riot. Together, they threw a lot of parties, at which criminals and
> jazz musicians and black men would be present, and they had love
> affairs, listened to Elvis Presley. Some of them dabbled in
> chicanery, some made exotic marriages, some turned homosexual.
> ... It all made marvellous copy for the gossip columns, who
> reported each fresh extravagance and invented something called
> the Chelsea Set.[5]

Cammell's world intersected with this Chelsea set and it is easy to see in
the mid-50s the protean shape of the elements that would become
Performance in the late 60s. In particular the fascination with crime and
pop music as well as ambivalent sexualities had already been well
established. But Cammell tired of the Chelsea set and left London for
New York looking for a truly modern life and art.

The precise dissatisfactions that drove Cammell from London (he
was never to return as a permanent resident) are impossible to
determine, but looking back it is easy to describe a life which had
reached a series of impasses. In 1954 he had married an extraordinarily
beautiful Greek actress called Maria Andipa but the marriage had ended
and ended acrimoniously with a pregnancy which Donald never
intended. Indeed, Donald was only ever to see his son once and
in leaving England he was leaving behind a family he had not
anticipated.

In a more speculative vein, New York may have beckoned as a
more cosmopolitan and bohemian city than London and one more likely
to accommodate Donald's sexual tastes. But his art was also increasingly
a source of dissatisfaction. The thought of becoming a successful society
portraitist appalled him and he found that the representational style he
had learnt in Annigoni's studio was increasingly inadequate. How long
he intended to stay in New York is uncertain but it was in this city, right
at the tail end of the 50s, that he met the beautiful young Texan model
Deborah Dixon with whom he was to live for most of the following
decade, and who was to work as costume designer on *Performance*.
When the couple returned to Europe in the early 60s, it was to Paris and
not to London. Cammell seems to have been determined to put England
behind him from his mid-twenties. Although he continued to visit

England often from Paris – it was on these visits that he was to meet the circle of people who were both to figure in and make *Performance* – he was never to base himself permanently there again. Los Angeles, where he had gone to finish editing *Performance* in 1969, was to be his final home until he killed himself in April 1996.

It is difficult to know exactly what prompted this voluntary exile. From one perspective, it corresponds to a search for artistic purpose. Society portraits, lucrative as they might have been, were quickly exhausted as a serious genre. When Cammell set out for New York he was trying out a very different style of painting, abstract and non-figurative. In Paris he went back to figurative painting; this time the subject matter was naked girls toying with each other rather than society beauties gazing out of the canvas. The themes he explored in this final painting stage were the dominant obsession of Cammell's life. As Marianne Faithfull puts it succinctly: 'That was Donald's thing. Threesomes.'[6] But it seems unlikely that the flight from England was simply because it was easier to get two girls into bed in New York or Paris although this probably shouldn't be ignored as a contributing factor.

Perhaps most importantly New York and then Paris offered an escape from the class system that so rigidly rules British society. In many ways, Cammell always remained a privileged member of the British upper class. But his lineage, both Scottish and artistic, created a distance from the Chelsea set. The gossip columns might make them appear wild and subversive; in reality they were lodged within class relations as secure as they were ancient. To Cammell they may have seemed hopelessly trapped. Cammell rarely talks about class in his many interviews but his only return to England to work was at a time, 1968, in which the old fetters of class seemed to be loosening, and it was to make a film which celebrated that emancipation.

Whatever the reasons, it was in Paris in the mid-60s as he turned thirty that Cammell was to opt for film as his medium of choice, to abandon painting and to set himself on the path that was to lead to *Performance*. The abandonment of painting is perhaps easier to understand than the choice of film as his new medium. Since he had tired of portrait painting, he had been unable to make a living as a painter and while Deborah Dixon's successful career as a model was enough to support them easily, simple economic considerations would have suggested that brush and easel had had their day. More important was

Cammell's growing conviction that painting was a dead medium which had reached its zenith with Impressionism and which was now finished. This intellectual position may well have been the rationalisation of a simple dislike of the art in which he had been encouraged since he was a small boy of three. Deborah Dixon remains convinced that he didn't like painting and that it was a relief for him to give it up.

Film in Paris in the mid-60s was the art of the moment and cinema was part of the world in which Dixon and Cammell moved. Indeed Cammell has a walk-on part in Eric Rohmer's *La Collectionneuse* (1966). But it is strange that in accounts of his life at that time film plays a very minor role. That he went to the cinema is certain but his passions were all literary: Borges and Burroughs, Genet and Artaud. When he contributed a list of ten favourite films to a *Time Out* poll in the 90s, it is striking that not one of them is from this period of the mid- to late 60s in which he made the change from painting to film: Stanley Kubrick's *Dr Strangelove* (1963), Mike Leigh's *Naked* (1993), Jean-Luc Godard's *Nouvelle vague* (1990), Murakami's *Tokyo Decadence Topaz* (1991), Ridley Scott's *Blade Runner* (1982), Bernardo Bertolucci's *The Conformist* (1969), Sergei Eisenstein's *Ivan the Terrible* (1942–6), Akira Kurosawa's *Throne of Blood* (1957) and Luis Buñuel's *The Discreet Charm of the Bourgeoisie* (1972). Only Eisenstein, Kurosawa and Kubrick predate *Performance*, and if the *nouvelle vague* appears it is in the extraordinary and obscure Godard film of the 90s rather than any of the films that Cammell might have been expected to see in Paris of the 60s. It is also striking that Cammell's early scripts are written entirely in novelistic form without any indication of camera angles or perspective. Even the script for *Performance* which Warner Bros. were to finance gives no indication of camera position although it, unlike its predecessors, is written in conventional film script form.

If film seems to have left him curiously untouched, Cammell was developing what were to be a series of intellectual obsessions. The first and most important of these was sex. In every account of Donald Cammell by every friend and acquaintance sex figures as a dominating theme. And not just any sex: specifically the threesomes that Marianne Faithfull describes as 'Donald's thing'. Myriam Gibril, Cammell's girlfriend in the early 70s, recounts how this obsession had its roots in the late 50s when Cammell came back to his Chelsea studio to find his then girlfriend in bed with her sister. The invitation to join them was one

of the defining moments in Cammell's life. According to Marianne
Faithfull, he and Deborah Dixon were to have scenes with both Anita
Pallenberg and Michèle Breton and from this perspective Turner can be
understood as a self-portrait.

But Cammell was not a rock star. He was, however, acutely aware
of and interested in the phenomenon. It is doubtful if anyone has yet
fully measured the significance and impact of that moment in the history
of the black Atlantic when the descendants of the slaves who had been
shipped from the barracoons sent back through the city (which had built
its fortune on their ancestors' bodies) the music which a generation of
white working-class youth was to use to articulate its desires and
depressions. It is true that the 60s was a time of sex and drugs and rock
and roll but the greatest of these was rock and roll because it was
through the music that the other pleasures found their articulation.

It is almost impossible to recall the excitement and astonishment of
that time when the Beatles, the Rolling Stones, the Who, the Kinks and
the Animals plus thousands of other more transient names burst out of
the pubs and clubs of Liverpool, London and Newcastle. Indeed it is still
probably too soon to register the ultimate impact of this music. To
understand fully the interplay of class and culture, education and
pleasure which is involved in the phenomenon of pop music, that mixture
of electronic technology, African-American rhythms and contemporary
consumerism, is beyond the scope of this or any other single book. For
our purposes, suffice to say that the early 60s saw the first major
revolution in popular culture since the Second World War and that the
Chelsea set, of which Cammell had remained an overseas member, was
as affected by this new music and its culture as any other part of Britain.
One of the most striking features of this new music was how it catapulted
young, mainly working-class men through the barriers of class and
money with a rapidity which has almost no historical parallel. What has
no historical parallel whatsoever was that, on the other side of the class
divide, there were young men and women eager to embrace these
newcomers as equals. There were no headlines that announced that the
Rolling Stones had met the Chelsea set in 1964 (those were to come in 1967
with the Redlands drug bust) but meet they did and Donald Cammell,
fascinated by this new London scene was to start coming over more
frequently from Paris, above all to observe the goings on at 1 Courtfield
Road where Brian Jones and Anita Pallenberg held court.

If the new scene of rock began to fascinate him, there was an older obsession – one that Turner says in the film has 'been on the road a million years. And for a million years people have been coming in and dragging in to watch it.' Cammell was fascinated by violence and particularly by criminal violence. This fascination was part and parcel of the Chelsea set – no party was complete without a villain or two – but in Paris Cammell found the poet of this world: Jean Genet.

Genet's autobiographical novels, which trace his criminal life and his adoration for the muscular thugs who inhabited it, had been seized on by Sartre in the 50s as offering the perfect example of the existentialist hero, the man determined to live from one moment to the next and refuse any definition of himself by his past. So impressed was Cammell by Genet that he gave copies of Genet's *The Thief's Journal* to both James Fox and Mick Jagger to read as preparation for *Performance*. In an early draft of the script, Cammell introduces Chas with the following description:

> Chas is the top 'Front Man' of Harry Flowers' firm. He's a criminal, a young thug, who's been picked for this key job by the professionals who run the business because he is what he is. In the first pages of THE THIEF'S JOURNAL, Jean Genet describes to perfection the essence of his kind:
>
>> Crime, I said to myself, had a long wait before producing such perfect successes as Pilorge and Angel Sun … it was necessary that a host of circumstances concur: to the handsomeness of their faces, to the strength and elegance of their bodies there had to be added their taste for crime, the circumstances which make the criminal, the moral vigour capable of accepting such a destiny, and finally, punishment, its cruelty, the intrinsic quality which enables a criminal to glory in it.
>
> In a sociologist's view, psychopaths. But it is equally true that Mr Genet's vision is equally true, if not truer. Of course, he loved young men like this with a pure and powerful love. Possibly this is where it is, to coin a phrase, at. In any case Genet takes for granted the essence of Chas; which is, not to be violent, *but to be violence*. (Not to kill – a gun going off; but to threaten death – a loaded gun.)

I give the name violence to a boldness lying idle and hankering for danger. … It unnerves you. This violence is a calm that disturbs you. One sometimes says: 'A guy with class'. Pilorge's delicate features were of an extreme violence. Their delicacy in particular was violent. … Even when at rest, motionless and smiling, there escaped from them through the eyes, the nostrils, the mouth, the palm of the hand … a radiant and sombre anger visible as a haze.

Sex and drugs, rock and roll and violence – when Cammell decided to write for the cinema in the mid-60s almost all the ingredients for *Performance* were in place. Although Cammell's early scripts before *Performance* all include violence, the violence lacks all conviction and reality. It wasn't until he located that violence in the criminal world of London's East End – the world of the Kray brothers – that his writing took on a wholly new power.

The Touchables (1968) told the story of a rock star kidnapped by young female fans who tantalise and torture him for his attention. The script, which came from an idea of Cammell's younger brother David, was handed over to Ian La Fresnais and resulted in another forgettable 'swinging London' movie. More important for the future was *Duffy* (1968), which was a heist movie in which two brothers plan to swindle their father with the help of an engaging American hippy, the eponymous Duffy played by James Coburn. The film, which Cammell wrote with Harry Joe Brown Jnr, son of a famous Hollywood producer, started life with the French title '*Avec Avec*', a gambling term. The original script was set in the world of young hip Parisians and involved crime, double-dealing and sexual shenanigans. This brief description suggests a film with many of the same themes and motifs as *Performance*, but it is difficult to recognise this in the movie that Columbia produced and Robert Parrish directed entitled *Duffy*. The *Monthly Film Bulletin* was accurate: 'When hippydom gets the Midas touch from Hollywood finance, it's predictable that the result should be embarrassing if not downright painful.'[7] Nobody felt the pain more than Cammell himself. As he had watched his hip script transform itself into a laughable Hollywood version of swinging Europe, he had complained with more and more vehemence. Eventually he was thrown off the set. Thus was born his determination to direct.

Duffy was also important in relation to *Performance* because one of the parts was played by the young British actor James Fox. Cammell already knew Fox from the new mid-60s version of the Chelsea set. The King's Road was now a centre of international attention rather than simply the smartest end of Bohemian London. The most significant element in this globalisation of London was music and Fox was, to use the vernacular of the time, tuned in. In Los Angeles, while filming *The Chase* (1966), Fox had taken up with an ex-girlfriend of Lenny Bruce who had introduced him to the burgeoning world of Californian rock and roll. Back in London and now with Andee Cohen, the couple were spending much of their time with Mick Jagger and Marianne Faithfull. As Fox and Cammell bemoaned what was happening with *Duffy*, they agreed that they would work together again on another Cammell project.

Through *Duffy* and its director, Robert Parrish, Cammell also met Sandy Lieberson, then an agent for CMA (Creative Management Agency). Lieberson too was connected to Chelsea as he had sought to represent both Marianne Faithfull and the Rolling Stones in their embryonic film careers. Lieberson, a native of Los Angeles, had set out for an orthodox career in business but in the mid-50s after two years in the Navy had opted for the entertainment business. He first worked as an agent for William Morris and in 1961 he had moved to Rome for CMA. He came to London because CMA had signed Peter Sellers and as part of the deal had to set up an office there. Lieberson thus arrived in a London buzzing with the sound of the 60s. As an agent he was fascinated by the possibilities offered by these new young gods of pop music. But he was also fascinated by the phenomenon of 60s London itself, and in particular the character of Cammell, 'who was not like anybody that I had met before'. So struck was Lieberson by Cammell that he had no hesitation in telling him he should not just write but also direct the movie that they soon planned to do together. Thus an agent who had never produced a film encouraged a novice screenwriter to take on the exacting role of director.

The film they were planning was a film which would mix crime and the new world of pop. The film was to be called 'The Liars' and was to star Marlon Brando as a criminal on the run and Mick Jagger as the pop star in whose house he ends up. Cammell had met the actor years before in Paris when Brando was acting in *The Young Lions* (1958) and they had kept in touch; indeed Brando was to play a major and destructive role in Cammell's life after *Performance*.

'The Liars' (a 69-page draft of which survives in Sandy Lieberson's papers) tells a story which is both familiar and foreign, a tame ur-tale which has none of the power of its ferocious offspring. The first third of the film is set in Paris where Cotrelli, a Brooklyn hood, has arrived to carry out a contract killing. In his escape from the scene of the crime, Cotrelli, the supreme professional, forgets his ticket which has written on it an incriminating name and telephone number. As the police close in on him at the airport, his only possibility of escape is to take a plane to the nearest city to Paris and hope that he can go to ground there. London is the city which becomes his unwilling destination. Once there and unable to register in a hotel, he finds himself in Earl's Court the only place his cab driver can suggest where he might find rented accommodation outside normal hours. Here Cotrelli rents a room from a reclusive musician called Haskin in a flat which also houses a runaway teenage girl, Simon. Haskin is a musician who has resigned from the hit group the Spinal Chords (a title that recurs in early drafts of *Performance* as Turner's backing band) because he disagrees with their decision to produce commercial music. While Simon falls in love with Cotrelli as they spend the day together, Haskin goes on a tour of Chelsea and Soho taking in all the sights of swinging London and picking up Pherber, a multi-national groupie *avant la lettre*, with whom he ends up in both bed and bath.

The existing draft ends inconclusively, indeed it doesn't so much end as just stop. While the very barest outline of the *Performance* plot – gangster on the run seeks refuge in rock musician's flat – is present, the existing script bears much more of a resemblance to Cammell's first two efforts than it does to *Performance*. One of the more ludicrous aspects of films of the mid-60s, both American and British, is the attempt to capture youth culture in general and 'swinging London' in particular. It has to be said that 'The Liars' reads as though it would have been another lamentable contribution to the genre, a worthy successor to *The Touchables*. The gangster is an off-the-shelf American hitman and, while the opening is inventive, there is hardly a hint of the genuine investigation of violence. Only a few lines towards the end as Cotrelli handles his gun suggest something more:

> He blows an invisible speck of dust off the backsight, empties the magazine, opens the breech, squints down the barrel, and then with

the concentration of a man practising a well-proven self-therapy, he starts to take the damn thing to pieces, checking each segment of the mechanism with fanatic punctiliousness.

He already looks much calmer.

Haskin, the musician, is equally banal: a paint-by-numbers character who steals food and records rather than sell out his music. The only really vital figure in the whole story is Pherber. In fact her name changes three times in the course of the script from Pilar to Phoebe to Pherber but at all times she exudes a vital force and energy. When the Supremes come on the car record player, she pushes the reject button instantaneously: 'These fucking Supremes, they really need to be gang-raped, you know?' The tones are unmistakably those of Anita Pallenberg as is also the general description of this German-Italian jet-setter who may decide next year to be English. In a late interview Cammell was to say that Pallenberg was one of the great influences on *Performance* – she is certainly the first recognisable character to take form.

Brando passed on this very early script and Cammell wrote a new version titled, 'The Performers'. This script bears only the faintest of resemblances to 'The Liars' and, despite numerous differences from the final film, is clearly a script for the film we know. The gangster on the run has metamorphosed into a contemporary Londoner, Chas Devlin, working for a gang boss obviously based on Ronnie Kray. The house in which he takes refuge (now significantly located in Notting Hill rather than Earl's Court) is inhabited by a rock recluse, driven by much more complex motives than making music which is commercially pure.

It was this story, if not this script, that persuaded James Fox and Mick Jagger to agree to appear in Cammell's film and at this point Cammell and Sandy Lieberson had what looked like a serious deal: there was, however, one further component before the package was complete. Cammell had already decided that he wanted Nicolas Roeg to be the cinematographer. In a pattern which repeats itself time and again, it is probable that Roeg's most important qualification was that he knew Cammell socially; Cammell at one stage had wanted to paint Roeg's first wife Susan Stevens, and Roeg moved in many of the same circles as Cammell. But Roeg was also arguably the best cinematographer working in Britain at that time. For Lieberson Roeg was an inspired choice. If the financiers complained about Donald's inexperience he could simply point to the experienced cinematographer who would guide the tyro director through his paces.

Roeg started his career as a 19-year-old in Marylebone Studio making tea and dubbing French films. By the end of the 50s he was working as a director of photography himself and in the 60s he registered one of the greatest photographic achievements in the history of British cinema with his work on Corman's *The Masque of the Red Death* (1964), as well as providing unforgettable lighting in Truffaut's *Fahrenheit 451* (1966) and Schlesinger's *Far From the Madding Crowd* (1967). When Cammell approached him, Roeg was about to direct his first feature *Walkabout* (1970). He told Cammell he was now only interested in lighting films if he was also directing. Cammell immediately suggested that Roeg co-direct with him. Roeg hesitated for some weeks but the attraction of the project and the postponement of *Walkabout* led him to accept.

Perhaps the most frequent and least interesting question asked about *Performance* is whether the film was 'really' Roeg's or 'really' Cammell's. In the 70s, as Roeg went on to make a succession of successful and striking films, *Performance* was often credited to him alone. When Cammell finally got one of his own scripts off the ground in the late 80s, *Performance* began to be seen as his film. And since his suicide in 1996, Cammell is increasingly credited as the 'true' author. To understand why any attempt to so attribute the film is deeply misleading takes us to the heart of *Performance*.

In the terms in which the question is asked, the simplest research reveals it to be mistaken. Once the decision to work together had been taken, Roeg and Cammell functioned as one. Although there were to be serious disagreements when Cammell went off to Los Angeles to re-edit the film to Warner Bros. instructions, for the period that they were working together Roeg and Cammell seemed literally, in imitation of Chas and Turner, to fuse and to merge. Roeg looks back on that period as 'a sort of secret exploration of our own brains' when their 'personal egos fused into one', when they were 'so secretly close' and they 'supported each other in manipulation'. It was, says Roeg, who clearly finds it painful to remember, 'more than a movie', it was a process in which 'without anybody knowing we changed our minds about life'.

Roeg's painful recall of a blissful period of collaboration is confirmed by almost all the other witnesses from that period. Most of the actors involved in the film remember Roeg's and Cammell's endless conversations on the set, their script-writing sessions each evening, their almost telepathic communication. Cammell, in an interview given not long before his death, spoke candidly of the division of labour at which they arrived. Cammell concerned himself with the actors while Roeg's primary attention was on the camera and its positioning. Each night they would discuss the next day's shoot, Cammell explaining his visual ideas and Roeg talking about the performances.

It might seem sufficient to stop here, to accept that the film was the work of these two men and to leave the question at that. But the reason the question of the 'authorship' of *Performance* is so irrelevant is that the genius of Cammell and Roeg was to allow an almost unprecedented level of creative contribution to the film they were making. They gathered the sounds and images of London in that unforgettable year of 1968 as the city seemed poised between an old and a new world and they delivered a picture and a soundtrack of that moment. From the Thomas a Becket in south London to the Pheasantry in the King's Road, it was their ability to let both people and things find their own voice and angle which makes *Performance* the greatest British film ever made.

If this is indeed the genius of *Performance* then it is even possible to make a perverse argument that the real author of the film was David Litvinoff. Even more than his great friend Christopher Gibbs, in whose house he was to kill himself – 'the ultimate discourtesy', Gibbs murmured to me when I interviewed him – it was Litvinoff who provided the bridge between the world of the Kray twins and the Rolling Stones. It was Litvinoff who ensured that the range the film covered; that the intersections of class and sex that it explored; the complicities of violence and society that it revealed, were much greater than any predecessor or successor.

David Litvinoff is one of the great mythic characters of 60s London. A monomaniacal fantasist who made up believable fictions as easily as he recounted unbelievable truths, it is more than difficult to discover the real facts of his extraordinary life. According to Gibbs he came from a large family of Russian Jews in the East End and several of his bothers, including the writer Emmanuel Litvinoff, became extremely successful in a variety of professions. Litvinoff, or Litz as he was known, chose a very different path determined in part by his sexuality. A suppressed, violent buttoned-up homosexual who hung out with street boys, Litvinoff was as likely to be found in an East End pub drinking with the Krays, in a Soho pinball arcade picking up errant schoolboys, or at the Markham Arms, centre of the Chelsea set, adding a spice of violence and mystery to the cocktail of crème de menthe, sex and tabloid headlines which characterised that world as it took shape in the late 50s. Both James Fox and David Cammell remember meeting Litvinoff in Soho as schoolboys. Fox remembers him as a kind of latter-day Fagin teaching schoolboys to pinch cigarettes. Cammell recalls meeting him as autumn turned into winter and Litvinoff remarking that he looked cold. Two days later he turned up at the Cammell household with a magnificent scarlet-lined jacket as a present. Five years later David was embarrassed when a fellow guest at a dinner party admired the jacket and remarked that he had had an identical one stolen some five years ago. How Litvinoff supported himself is one of those mysteries to which no one can provide an answer but both gambling and theft seem likely sources. He was also, by every account, one of the century's great talkers; a Coleridge who neglected to commit anything to paper. London rumour claims that tapes exist of Litvinoff in full flow but they prove elusive, a sort of technological abominable snowman, always attested to at second-hand: I knew a man who knew a man who heard them. Perhaps most significantly of all, Litvinoff was a genuine member of the horrifically violent world of the Krays. Once having fallen out with the terrifying twins (a gambling debt, a row with Ronnie over boys?), he opened his door to be swiftly punched unconscious. When he came to he was hanging upside down from the railings of the building where he lived, with his head shaved completely bare.[8] He didn't just take it, he also handed it out. After the Rolling Stones Redlands bust, where the police had obviously been tipped off by an informer, suspicion fell on an inoffensive hanger-on, Nicky Kramer. It was Litz who took it upon

himself to go round and beat Kramer to a pulp in the interests of establishing that Kramer had nothing to do with the tip-off.

To claim Litvinoff as the author of *Performance* is a perverse gesture of irritation with the tedious and falsely knowing question: was it Roeg or was it Cammell? But it is undoubtedly the case that the real history of *Performance* begins when Cammell, having abandoned the American hood who was to provide a role for Brando, decided instead to take his gangster from one of the worlds that Litvinoff inhabited and to which he could provide access for his hip Chelsea friends. In the summer of 1967 Cammell holed himself up in a small Chelsea flat with Litvinoff. It is from this moment that one can date the history of *Performance*. On the final film Litvinoff was credited as Dialogue Consultant and Technical Advisor.[9]

It is one of the sager of Hollywood nostrums that to make one successful film you have to make five: the film you script, the film you cast, the film you shoot, the film you edit and the film you release. Let us now follow *Performance* through these five stations.

THE SCRIPT

. . . .

Performance opens with a credit sequence which cuts between a black Rolls Royce driving through the countryside and a couple making love with whips and mirrors. Sexual business completed, the man, Chas Devlin (James Fox), hurries his partner Dana (Ann Sidney) out of his flat. He then prepares himself for his daily round which is to provide the muscle for his boss Harry Flowers' (Johnny Shannon) protection business. As he terrifies a mini-cab firm and a strip club, we cut back and forth to a court sequence in which a defence lawyer, while expatiating on the ethics of business and society, threatens to name Harry Flowers as the real author of the crimes for which his client is charged. Chas together with his sidekicks Rosebloom (Stanley Meadows) and Moody (John Bindon) warn Flowers' erstwhile associate that naming Flowers will result in grievous bodily harm. The lawyer (Allan Cuthbertson), who proves to be the owner of the black Rolls Royce, is outraged and demands that 'you address your remarks to me'. Taking him at his word, the next morning Chas and his gang ambush the lawyer's chauffeur, destroy the Rolls with acid and leave the chauffeur tied to the ruins of the car, having shaved his head.

In the meantime we have been introduced to the world of Harry Flowers, where Chas' brutality is represented in a series of euphemisms of which the key term is 'performer'. Flowers' entire language is made up of a series of metaphors from the world of business with a constant undertone of perverted, specifically homosexual, sex. The lawyer dealt with, Flowers turns to the next step in the expansion of his business empire: the forced acquisition of Joey Maddox's (Antony Valentine) betting shop. Chas, for the first time in the film, becomes animated in his desire to deal with 'that slag Joey' with whom he obviously has some deep and ancient connection. Flowers forbids Chas to have anything to do with Joey, claiming that, for Chas, the matter is 'double personal'. He instructs Rosey to have the betting shop demolished. Disobeying Flowers' instructions, it is Chas who goes to pick up Joey from the wreckage of his shop. He delivers Joey to the meeting with Flowers where the merger (a key word in the film) is completed. At the meeting Flowers makes clear his displeasure at Chas' refusal to obey his orders. When Chas returns to his flat that night he is ambushed by Joey and two friends who beat him within an inch of his life as they try to force him to admit that he is a 'poof' (while the exact relationship between Chas and Joey is never clear, it undoubtedly involves past homosexual experiences). Half-dead, Chas manages to escape his tormentors and to get his hands on a concealed gun. Slowly and with great deliberation he shoots Joey through the head.

Chas is now in mortal danger. When he phones his boss it is swiftly apparent that he has become an embarrassment to the 'firm' and that if they find him they will kill him. Desperate for somewhere to hide Chas sets out for an aunt in Barnstaple. Waiting for a train at Paddington he overhears a black musician, Noel, telling his mother how he has just left his room in Powis Square owing back rent. Sensing an opportunity, Chas turns up at the house claiming to be a juggler friend of Noel's and offering to pay the back rent. He is welcomed into the house by the stunningly beautiful Pherber (Anita Pallenberg) who begins teasing him in a bizarre sexual game which will continue throughout the second half of the film. The house we soon learn belongs to a reclusive rock star, Turner (Mick Jagger), who lives there with his two girlfriends Pherber and Lucy (Michèle Breton) in a private world of sybaritic indulgence in sex and drugs looked after by Mrs Gibbs and her precocious young daughter (Laraine Wickens).

A business disagreement: gang boss Harry Flowers with Chas Devlin and the new and reluctant associate Joey Maddocks

Turner is at first unwilling to rent the room to Chas, but realising that the gangster has the power and confidence as a performer that he himself now lacks, he agrees to let him stay. The final third of the film juxtaposes Chas' attempt to organise his escape to America via telephone calls to his cousin Tony (Kenneth Colley) with Turner's and Pherber's exploration of Chas' psyche as they feed him hallucinogenic mushrooms and play increasingly complicated sexual and psychic games with him. The climax of this night of excess finds Chas accepting sexual advances from all three of the inhabitants in Powis Square but also forgetting to make a crucial phone call to Tony to pick up his false passport. This lapse allows Rosebloom (Rosey) and Moody to locate his hiding place.

Liberated from the cripplingly rigid masculinity that has ruled his every action, Chas makes tender love to Lucy and talks to her with an affection and direction that is completely new. But nemesis is at hand and Chas finds himself trapped in the house by Rosey and the chaps intent on killing him. He tells them that he must say goodbye to Turner and enters the rock star's bedroom. Turner asks to come with him but Chas tells the singer that he doesn't know where he's going. 'Yes I do,' replies Turner, and at this moment Chas turns, draws his pistol and shoots him through the head. The camera follows the bullet through Turner's head out through the roof of the house and follows Chas from behind as he is escorted towards the white Rolls Royce in which Harry Flowers is waiting. 'Hallo Chas,' says Harry as the performer gets into the car. As the Rolls draws away it is Turner's face that looks out the window.

There are two versions of the script of *Performance* written after the abandoned version with an American gangster. Although they are very different from the finished film they are clearly related to it. Most significantly they are written with a power and intensity completely missing from 'The Liars' or Cammell's previous scriptwriting efforts.

The first half of the film is well established in both scripts. The major surprise is that Chas' exploits as a performer which are shown in fast cutting montage in the film are revealed in the scripts in conventional sequences. More surprising still, the barrister (Harley-Brown) and his defence in court do not act as a counterpoint to Chas' actions. In the earlier scripts Harley-Brown is simply another of Chas' tasks. The barrister has been gambling at a club which Harry Flowers protects. One of Chas' regular chores is to collect such debts which are assigned to a

Flowers' company. The scene where Chas makes clear to the lawyer that he will have to pay his debt takes place inside the Garrick club and rivals any scene included in the film in the chilling violence of Chas' performance. The opening exchange of barbed pleasantries in the wood panelled room comes to an end with the following sequence:

A pause. HARLEY-BROWN puts down his glass, rises with dignity. As he does so, CHAS picks up the glass.

HARLEY-BROWN: Mr Devlin. I think you – (you had better be off now).

CHAS runs the diamond in his ring across the surface of the glass in his hand as he cuts off HARLEY-BROWN.

CHAS: Don't interrupt. You interrupt me again –

CHAS breaks off a section of the glass as he speaks, holding it delicately in his fingers.

CHAS: – and I'll cut your tongue out.

The class antagonism which is strong in the scene with the lawyer in the film is even stronger here. Chas' contempt both for the lawyer and his club is manifest in his every word and gesture. By the time their conversation is finished the lawyer is a man working on autopilot shocked right out of his social existence by the naked violence which Chas embodies. It is at this point, when he has totally established his superiority, that Chas finally apes his betters and in a show put on for other members who have just entered the room tells Harley-Brown, in mock upper-class accent, how much he is looking forward to joining the club.

If the film lacks some of the raw class antagonism of this scene, it gains much by making Harley-Brown the lawyer who is about to name Harry Flowers in court. In the film Harley-Brown is not a shady barrister keen to use his social position and his knowledge of the law to escape his gambling debts. He represents the Law in its full psychic authority and class power. Narratively it also has the advantage of establishing a world of tabloid publicity which Flowers is desperate to avoid and which is the greatest threat posed by Chas' subsequent murder of Joey. More importantly it allows the lawyer to have his day in court with a speech which provides the most general social context for the events that are about to unfold before our eyes. Significantly this speech introduces the theme of 'merging' which, in both its economic and psychic forms, is so key to the film. If the first half deals with forced and false mergers in which sex and power are used but disavowed, it is inevitable that it should end with a shooting which entails extinction. The merger of the second half of the film recognises and celebrates the power of sex and ends with a shooting which creates a new hybrid being.

The second half of the film, in these early scripts, is very different from the finished film. If the inhabitants of Powis Square are all already clearly delineated and named, the house is not the hermetically sealed alternative social and psychic space that it is in the film. Characters come and go and even Turner leaves the house. Mrs Gibbs has a much more significant role and Turner has an assistant (Mojo).[10] More importantly the narrative crux of the second half of the film is a police bust in which Turner allows the police to discover his drugs in order to protect Chas from the search that would reveal his gun.

The scripts do, however, make clear the direction of Cammell's thought particularly in the scene where Chas and Turner talk after the police bust:

> They say various things, which I cannot explain now, and others which I cannot yet know. Before this point in this adventure is reached (by me, you, them) it will be apparent that these two have had, in the interminable thirteen hours that have passed since they met, a considerable effect on each other.
>
> They say various things ... it is unlikely, for example that CHAS would ask, 'Why have you helped me, Turner?' ... in words, that is. For in a certain way, he does ask. And in another way, equally clear, TURNER will answer him.
>
> Being TURNER, if he said, 'Well the fact is, I believe in Universal Love,' he would make it sound profoundly ironic.

In the script these words are so hedged around with brackets and grammatical qualifications that it is clear Cammell is desperately searching for a language that he will only find in the film when Chas offers Turner the ultimate act of gratitude. But they do make clear that Chas and Turner are intended to make a fundamental connection. But the form and nature of that connection is not even hinted at in the scripts. Both end with Chas being driven away to his death as Turner watches from a window.

Even clearer are the comments after Chas and Lucy make love just before Rosey and the chaps arrive:

> Something in CHAS has changed. Perhaps, though, his screwed up ego would refuse to face the fact that for a little while anyway, he is not trying to demonstrate that he is 'nothing but a man'. Perhaps he has realised that these three people are not concerned with the demonic and pathetic problems of gender that rot the human race ... that they don't waste their lives and loves trying to define their sexes. Relieved of this duty he is marvellously at ease. LUCY is happy too. She says things to him in French. He understands perfectly.

If the script suggests much of the power of the film, particularly in the early dialogue, it also makes clear how far Cammell was from realising his goal, or even, in the second half, whether his goal was yet clear to him. What is certain is that his and Roeg's task would be heavily dependent on the casting.

THE CAST

. . . .

Rarely can a film have been more perfectly cast. While it would be stupid to discount the fine judgment that Cammell and Roeg brought to this task, it is also important to realise, as with almost all films, how large a part was to be played by luck. If James Fox and Mick Jagger were part of the very premises of the film, Anita Pallenberg and Johnny Shannon were to bring to the screen elements of reality which had never before been recorded on film.

Jagger was the very condition of the film's existence. Over the years, Cammell had talked to Jagger about his film projects at the parties they both attended. It is easy, even across the gap of thirty years, to understand why Warner Bros. were keen to finance a film starring the lead singer of the Rolling Stones. The Stones had already established themselves as second only to the Beatles in the wave of music that had rolled out of Britain and round the world in the mid-60s. To cast a Stone, particularly if there was an album attached and the budget was kept to reasonable proportions, was a sure bet. It is more difficult, however, to re-create a moment in history when the Stones in general, and Jagger in particular, were seen as a positive menace to society, the unacceptable face of a youth culture which, to many, threatened the very fabric of civilisation. In retrospect, with Jagger as famous today for his business acumen and his love of cricket as for the excesses of his youth, and when youth culture is now best understood as part and parcel of the process of market segmentation, this fear seems ridiculous but at the time it was real. And in a more complex moment of evaluation, a moment of which *Performance* is a key part, the fear can look both ridiculous and real. Ridiculous because the young people who listened to rock and roll, took drugs, bought fashionable clothes and demonstrated against Vietnam were little concerned to genuinely challenge the 'straight' society which they mocked; and real because the boundaries of class and gender were suddenly up for renegotiation for the first time since Elizabethan London. In retrospect, and at the time, no one captured this ambivalence more fully than the Rolling Stones and no Stone embodied it better than their lead singer Michael Philip Jagger.

Whereas Brian Epstein transformed the Beatles from a raw, leather-clad rhythm and blues band, and sanitised them with Beatle suits, Beatle haircuts and pop music which hardly hinted at the blues, Andrew

Loog Oldham found the Stones and encouraged them to emphasise their long hair, their unkempt appearance and their roots in the music of urban black America. Thus runs the legend and there is enough truth in it to justify the Tom Wolfe epigram, 'The Beatles want to hold your hand, the Stones want to burn your town.' The Stones were 'edgy', the adjective that Jagger now uses to describe the entire 60s epoch, and nowhere was this edginess more evident than in the Redlands drug bust.

Redlands was Keith Richards' house in the country and it was there in February 1967 that the most famous drug bust of the decade took place.[11] The passage of thirty years and the publication of numerous memoirs and histories mean that we now know that the eight men and one woman the police arrested had spent an afternoon in that most English of pursuits, a country walk. True they had all been high as kites but it was still a far cry from the picture conjured up by the tabloid stories the next day. Soon everyone in England 'knew' that the police had interrupted a full-blown orgy featuring as its centrepiece the consumption of a Mars Bar which Marianne Faithfull had strategically placed to enhance the charm of her most private parts. The Mars Bar episode is one of the most fascinating of urban legends and no doubt some dedicated student of historical anthropology may well sketch out the complex mechanisms which turned this quiet afternoon into a scene of riot and excess. But one does not need much historical or technical knowledge to understand that what was largely at stake here was the image which Middle England projected on to Faithfull and her boyfriend Jagger. Marianne and Mick were parents' worst fantasies of what their children were going to become. For the children they were the promise that growing up might not be the total bore it had hitherto seemed. For generations parents had warned their children against 'bad companions', now those companions were on the front page of every paper and earning millions of pounds. Rock music, easily available on 45s to be played on ever cheaper gramophones, cannabis, available both from the new West Indian communities and from early hippy trade routes to Morocco, and sex, which the Pill made available with what seemed like total safety; all three opened up to teenagers forms of experience which were totally alien to their parents.

Thirty years on, the social implications of these innovations have only begun to be worked out, thirty years back it was easy to see the generation gap as a genuine civil war. The Stones, hugely popular and

Cecil Beaton on set with Fox and Jagger

clearly rebellious, were the frontline. When they were sentenced to jail after the Redlands bust – Richards for allowing his house to be used for the consumption of drugs, Jagger for the possession of a tiny quantity of amphetamines – it seemed that the war might erupt into revolution. If *The Times* editorial that used Pope's line, 'Who breaks a butterfly upon a wheel', as its title was part of an attempt to negotiate a ceasefire and if the release of the Stones on appeal confirmed the cessation of open hostilities, Jagger was, whether he liked it or not, the single most identifiable figure for whom sex and drugs were not just illicit pleasures but were a direct challenge to orthodox society. Jagger was thus not just another pop star (the thought with which Warner Bros. executives might have consoled themselves), he was the very sign of transgression. Cammell, who met him within the circles of the Chelsea set which we have already encountered (Christopher Gibbs and the art-dealer Robert Fraser, a key figure for this piece of social history, were both at the Redlands bust), had long talked to him about appearing in a film and indeed Jagger is the only person other than Sandy Lieberson who was already involved with the American hit-man version. But Cammell must have been aware, as he sat down in the summer of 1967 with David Litvinoff to write 'The Performers', that Jagger's power and image were expanding to include a whole generation. It is hardly suprising that Cammell initially chose to make a drug bust the centrepiece of the second half of the film and the police behaviour seems closely modelled on Redlands. In fact, this second half was jettisoned before shooting began but a reference to Redlands remains when Chas arrives at Powis Square and rings on the doorbell. Glancing down at the milk bottle crate he notices not only mushroooms but Mars Bars.

The in-joke is unimportant: what does matter is that in casting Jagger, Cammell had access to an entire national fantasy. Every star embodies roles and struggles which stretch out far beyond the world of entertainment but rarely does a film bring to the screen for the first time the living image of an entire range of new social forces.

By the time he seriously addressed himself to *Performance* Cammell had his other male lead in place, the friend he had made on *Duffy*: James Fox. Fox was that rare creature: a great British actor who was also a genuine film star. A child actor of a showbiz family, his father was an agent his mother an actor, he combined a conventional upper-class schooling at Harrow with serious roles in *The Miniver Story* and

The Magnet (1950). When he had completed his National Service, this beautiful young man moved effortlessly to success after success. Escorting his girlfriend Sarah Miles to the premiere of *The L-Shaped Room* (1962), he was spotted by Dirk Bogarde, then in pre-production on Joseph Losey's *The Servant* (1963). Fox was cast in the role of Tony, the decadent young gentleman who is destroyed and humiliated by his servant played by Bogarde. Wollen sees *The Servant* as one of the three films that form the intertext of *Performance* (the other two are Polanski's *Repulsion* (1965) and Antonioni's *Blowup* (1966)). Aside from the question of form and theme it is worth noting that there is a considerable overlap between these films. Fox's participation in *The Servant* is the most obvious, but, in addition, Polanski had been friendly with Cammell in Paris and Christopher Gibbs was to throw, in his Cheyne Walk apartment, the party which is one of the central scenes in *Blowup*.

Fox's role in *The Servant* made him an international star and in the next few years he was to take the lead in films as varied as Arthur Penn's *The Chase* (with Marlon Brando and Robert Redford) and Karel Reisz's *Isadora* (1968). If *The Chase* showed something of the range of which he was capable, the majority of Fox's roles were close to type: a handsome and rather ineffectual English aristocrat. To cast him as a brutal East End gangster showed either a preternatural instinct for his abilities or a touching innocence. In Cammell's case both elements were probably in play. That Fox wished to try something challenging is not surprising. His friend Cammell's charisma and his long acquaintance with Litvinoff may have helped give him confidence but it was Roeg who told the old Harrovian pretending to be working class that he must 'go away and come back as Chas'.

It was to the Thomas a Becket pub on the Old Kent Road that he went away and when he came back he was not only Chas but he had Harry Flowers with him. One of the many rumours that surround *Performance* is that Fox took the part so seriously that he suffered a nervous breakdown as a result. This story simplifies a much more complex tale. When Fox took on the role he was already a very troubled young man. In Rome the year before he had felt in his own words, 'morally disturbed', and he had also quit the set of *Isadora* before completing his final scene, preferring instead to disappear into the excesses of Rio's carnival. Marianne Faithfull's autobiography has recounted how closely the mind games of *Performance* were mirrored in

Jagger in full voice as Turner

the teasing and sexual friendship that she and Jagger enjoyed with Fox and his girlfriend Andee Cohen. And the teasing continued on the set of *Performance* where Jagger and Pallenberg in their different ways would mock Fox's 'straightness'. Mick, Anita and Jimmy thus redoubled the force fields that the film was creating between Turner, Pherber and Chas. Fox had broken up with Andee Cohen just before *Performance* went into production and he thus went through the rigours of the film without any close personal support. But it was not until well over a year after shooting finished, in December 1969, that he would end a period of profound solitude, tormented by feelings of unworthiness at his too easy success, by embracing Christianity and quitting acting for over a decade. *Performance* did not cause Fox to break down but it did capture him at a moment when he was living through the kind of confusion into which Chas is plunged once the door of 81 Powis Square is opened to him.

In casting Fox as Chas, Cammell was casting the biggest young star that Britain could boast. In casting an old Harrovian as an East End gangster, he was crossing class as transgressively as Pherber was to encourage Chas to cross gender. It was Litvinoff who had made this possible in the script, it was Litvinoff who now made it possible in performance. The Thomas a Beckett pub in south London was a legendary meeting ground between boxing and crime. It was in the gym above the pub that Henry Cooper trained for his world title fight with Mohammed Ali, and it was in the pub below that the criminals of south London would gather to reflect on their daily round. Litvinoff arranged through Tommy Gibbons, the pub owner, for Fox to stay in a little flat in Brixton. Each day Fox would train in the gym with the other boxers and each night he would drink with 'the chaps', a delightfully polite expression for the hardest of criminally hard men. His tutor in this brave new world was Johnny Shannon, a print worker who was also a boxing trainer on the side. Shannon was an ex-heavyweight boxer who had held amateur titles and had boxed with Joe Erskine and Henry Cooper in the Army. His first impression of Fox, with his hippy shirt, his long hair and his public school tones, was of a visitor from another society, if not another planet. But as Fox adopted an approved East End haircut, dressed in suits from the gangsters' favourite tailor in The Cut and worked out in the gym each day, he gradually crossed the great divide of British society. One night after they had been drinking into the early hours of the morning , Shannon remembers leaving the pub to find Fox's car blocked in the road. The 'chaps' had decided to have a laugh with their new-found friend. Fox merely mounted the pavement at speed, avoiding the car that was blocking the entrance and causing the pranksters to leap out of the way. Shannon remembers the salute they accorded Fox as he accelerated away as a real sign of acceptance.

It is an oft repeated tale in the writings on *Performance* that Fox became so immersed in his training for the role that he ended up going out with 'the chaps' for real. Both Fox and Shannon deny this categorically. The villains of the Thomas a Becket were far too professional to take out an amateur on what for them was strictly a job. What is undoubtedly true is that Fox became so thoroughly immersed in his role that he could be as frightening as Chas. There are clear memories of him going into the production office at the time and frightening the staff out of their wits. It is easy to see how this fear became rumour and transformed itself into legend, not least because the whole first part of the film is underwritten by the legend of the Krays.

Ronnie and Reggie Kray, twins from Hoxton in the East End, had become part of national mythology from the summer of 1964 when the

Sunday Mirror printed a story about a homosexual relationship between a leading London gangster and a peer of the realm. The peer in question, Lord Boothby, wrote to *The Times* identifying himself and denying everything, and was paid a substantial sum in damages by the *Sunday Mirror*. In fact, however, the story was largely true. Boothby knew Ronnie Kray and if their homosexual relationship was not direct, their shared taste for tough young men was integral to their association. Boothby had also used his influence to aid the twins in their criminal endeavours. From the time of the publication of a photograph picturing Boothby with a twin seated on either side of him, the Krays were the national image of violent crime, an image which lasts to this day and has survived Ronnie's death.[12] If the Krays were public property from 1964, they had been a tangential part of the Chelsea set for a longer time. In 1960 the twins, already a dominant force in the protection rackets of the East End, acquired a gambling club called Esmerelda's Barn in Wilton Place. It was here that many a late Chelsea night finished and a view of the ferocious twins was as much an attraction as the pleasure of losing one's money at the tables. As if to solidify the connection, Ronnie Kray moved into a Chelsea flat that he had acquired via a gambling debt and it was in Chelsea that he acknowledged publicly the homosexuality which had seemed like a bad secret in the East End but which was merely fashionable within a King's Road setting out to enjoy the 60s.

There is no doubt that in fashioning the figure of Harry Flowers, Cammell and Litvinoff had Ronnie Kray in mind. In retrospect one might wonder whether such a decision was more than a trifle dangerous. Kray was willing to resort to violence at the slightest insult, as Litvinoff had good cause to know. Perhaps they didn't care about the risks or perhaps Litvinoff knew Ronnie well enough to think he might be flattered. In any case shortly before the film started shooting the twins were arrested, making it impossible for them to interfere.

Their trial came early in 1969 and by the time it had finished the Krays had hugely increased their hold on the national imagination. The trial and the subsequent media industry which has specialised in the Krays have made them synonymous not simply with organised crime and brutal violence but also with a cockney East End of enormous vitality and amazing solidarity, a world which mocked a ruling class it did not recognise. *Performance* was to provide an image of that world and it was to do it not simply through the astonishing imaginative projection of

James Fox's Chas, a figure who managed to embody all the glamour of both upper-class actor and working-class character, but also through Johnny Shannon's Harry Flowers, where actor and character were much closer, where intonation and vocabulary did not have to be acquired but simply displayed.

Johnny Shannon, and particularly his voice, are at the very centre of *Performance*; a presentation of working-class London's confidence and arrogance which had never before reached cinema screens. Before *Performance* images of London crime derived from Dickens and other nineteenth-century novelists. Looking back to television shows such as *Dixon of Dock Green* and the Ealing films from which they borrow their image of the cockney criminal, one can only laugh at these innocently picturesque characters.[13] In *Performance* we hear the authentic twentieth-century tones of the Krays: the language of capitalist enterprise conjugated with euphemisms for violence to produce the industry of protection. The authenticity of this voice is the authenticity of Johnny Shannon.

Shannon was born in Lambeth in 1932 and his life before *Performance* had focused on the twin East End pursuits of boxing and 'the print'. If he was someone who stayed on the right side of the law, he moved none the less in the same world as the villains, 'the chaps'. He talked like them, he walked like them, he wore the same clothes, he drank the same drinks: he shared both their tastes and their accent. When he started to read the script with Jimmy Fox, it was entirely to help Fox get his accent right, but he soon found himself reading in front of Roeg and Cammell, in what, although Shannon didn't realise it, was an audition for the part of Chas' boss, Harry Flowers. When James Fox first suggested to Shannon that he might appear in the film, Shannon had assumed it would be the minor figure of the chauffeur; on learning the directors wanted him for a major role he was unworried because, as he now says, 'I didn't know there was anything to be worried about.'

The use of amateur actors or 'real people' in cinema is a device closely associated with Italian neo-realism. Its aesthetic justification is usually in terms of a fundamental commitment to realism and a dislike of the mannered affectations associated with certain schools of acting. However, it is probably more useful in looking at the early films of Rossellini and de Sica to think of the technique in terms of the presentation of social classes which have never before reached the screen. The force of Johnny Shannon's Harry Flowers in January 1971 when the film was released in London derived both from the novelty of the gestures he used and the tones he pronounced and from the fact that they were so different from the traditional representations of the cockney criminal; representations which were instantly rendered redundant. In fact it is difficult to recapture the shock of *Performance*'s first screenings. Shannon's own subsequent career and the host of imitations he spawned mean that the standardised representations of London crime are entirely derivative of this one film.

These developments should not obscure the fact that a great deal of the intensity of *Performance* derives from its totally original neo-realist representation of the London working class, a representation impossible to divorce from its use of genuine representatives of that class. In this respect the film's only precursor was Ken Loach and, in particular, his BBC film, *Up the Junction* (1967), based on the book by Nell Dunn which charted an upper-class Chelsea girl's investigation of the sexual and social possibilities offered by working-class Battersea. It is therefore entirely appropriate that Chas' sidekick Moody is played by John Bindon, for Bindon had been cast by Loach in his film, *Poor Cow* (1967), also based on a Nell Dunn novel, after Loach had overheard Bindon holding forth in a west London pub. Bindon, unlike Shannon, had already spent a lot of time in prison before he became an actor. He was to be charged with murder at the end of the 70s and violence punctuates the obituaries which followed his early death in October 1993. Shannon recalls that he had heard of him before the film because of a fight in which Bindon had bitten off his opponent's ear. Persuaded by his friends that he should return the ear, he presented it to his defeated antagonist in a cigarette box.

Alongside these two non-professionals, Cammell and Roeg cast as Rosebloom Stanley Meadows. Meadows was a familiar face from British television although just prior to *Performance* he had moved to France where he has worked ever since. But Meadows too came from an East End background and had spent much of his youth in the company of criminals. Like Shannon and Bindon he would continue to improve Litvinoff's dialogue right up to the final take.

If one understands the male casting in relation to notions of class and culture, crime and music, the female casting was about sex and nationality. There can be no doubt that from the very beginning Pherber was based on Anita Pallenberg. She dominates the textual history of the film as she dominated the 60s. Rarely central but always there, she was someone who seemed to be one step ahead of any game be it cultural or erotic, aesthetic or addictive. Her upbringing as a member of an aristocratic and artistic European family with connections in many countries had prepared her well for the international world of rock music and film. By the time she met the Rolling Stones she had already worked in Jasper Johns' studio, appeared in Schlöndorff's films and had been deeply affected by the Living Theatre. In London she already knew the art-dealer Robert Fraser and the ubiquitous Christopher Gibbs. She had also, almost by chance, developed a career as a model and through Deborah Dixon had met Donald Cammell.

Her move to London was, however, occasioned by her affair with that doomed figure Brian Jones. Brian Jones had been the dominant spirit in the Rolling Stones in the early days but by late 1965 when Anita moved in with him, this position was threatened both by the song-writing axis of Jagger and Richards and by Jones' increasingly fragile psychic state. But Pallenberg's arrival bought a remission from the disintegration which now threatened Jones and their house at Courtfield Road became

Anita Pallenberg, *the* beauty of the 60s

the centre for all kinds of experiments: musical, psychic and sexual.
Marianne Faithfull sets the scene in her memoir:

> Courtfield Road, Brian Jones and Anita Pallenberg's flat off
> Gloucester Road during the heady Paint-It-Black summer of 1966.
> … A veritable witches' coven of decadent illuminati, rock
> princelings and hip aristos. … Peeling paint, clothes, newspapers
> and magazines strewn everywhere. A grotesque little stuffed goat
> standing on an amp, two huge tulle sunflowers, a Moroccan
> tambourine, lamps draped with scarves, a pictographic painting of
> demons (Brian's?) and decorously draped over a tatty armchair, a
> legendary leg – Robert Fraser's, I should guess. There's Brian in
> his finest Plantagenet satins, fixing us with vacant fishy eyes. On the
> battered couch, an artfully reclining Keith is perfecting his
> gorgeous slouch. The hand gesturing in the manner of Veronese
> could only belong to the exquisite Christopher Gibbs, and
> hovering over the entire scene with single-lens-reflex-eye the
> invisibly ever-present photographer, Michael Cooper. At the
> centre like a phoenix on her nest of flames … the wicked Anita.[14]

A regular visitor at Coutfield Road was Donald Cammell and to his
friendship with Pallenberg was added a very close friendship with Jones.
When the couple split up in the spring of 1967 in Tangier with Richards
rescuing Pallenberg from an increasingly violent Jones, it was to
Cammell's flat in Paris that Jones fled. If there is a model for Turner, it
is probably Jones; a man destroyed by the success of his music and the
excess it brought in its wake; someone unable to find a way of living after
entering that psychic space reserved for ageing rock stars. But if Turner
is Jones, he is also Cammell and by casting Pallenberg who'd slept with
both, the film sets in play a dialectic of reality and representation which
allows it to investigate the interplay of sex and image more dangerously
than any commercial film before or since.

If Pallenberg was the obvious choice to play Pherber, she was not
the first. Tuesday Weld, the quintessential American bobby-soxer, who
was trying to make-over her image to include a great deal more grown-
up pursuits, came to London for the role. Her participation was brought
to an abrupt halt when Deborah Dixon tried some New Age therapy on
the back problem that was troubling the American actress and broke her

shoulder. It is close to impossible to imagine the film without Pallenberg. Her heart-stopping beauty, her extraordinary air of mystery as a figure both public and private, her legendary passage from one Stone to another and the possibility of a further passage to a third, all this is absolutely integral to the film; she is the guarantee that 81 Powis Square is real.

Another American actress, Mia Farrow, was also considered for a part but in what could look like an uncanny coincidence broke an ankle before she could even get on a plane to London. This second mishap allowed Cammell to suggest Michèle Breton as Lucy, the French waif who makes up Turner's *ménage à trois*. Once again this is casting from reality for the character of Lucy is obviously based on Breton herself. Cammell and Dixon had met Breton as a runaway kid in St Tropez where they summered and she had come to Paris to live with them. For Cammell she obviously represented the new youth of the 60s; the generation which had been formed by the music of Turner and his confrères and which now promised and threatened to make a new world in its image.

It is significant that none of the women considered for the film were English. The women in the film stand for a series of possibilities erotic and exotic which break the frigid and fetishised world of old England. To smash the barriers of class and gender, it is first necessary to rupture the identity of the nation: perhaps Pallenberg's and Breton's most important qualification is that they were, to use Chas' term, 'foreign'.

The casting of any movie is a complicated calculation of image and reality, of audience expectation and the possibilities of performance. Few films, however, can have thrown so much into the pot as *Performance*. The film presented the two most exciting aspects of contemporary London, pop music and crime, and, at the same time, it assembled a gathering of Cammell's friends and lovers. A sociological survey and a witches' brew.

THE SHOOT

. . . .

There can be few more legendary shoots than that of *Performance*. Even today there are still people in the film business in London who will tell you that the film was a disorganised mess because everybody involved was out of their heads on acid. Others speak of the live sex scenes which caused crew members to depart and labs to refuse to develop the material. Proof of this steamy material is to be found in the further legend that the out-takes from *Performance* won first prize at the Amsterdam Wet Dream festival in the autum of 1968. According to rumour, Keith Richards would prowl outside the set as Pallenberg's on-screen affair with Jagger came closer and closer to reality. Other stories recount how Robert Fraser was banned from the set for unspeakable behaviour; Jimmy Fox came apart at the seams as the film progressed and fled both set and industry when the film wrapped in order to rescue a soul torn apart by the demons that the film had invoked. Warner executives were so disturbed by the rushes of the bath scene that they closed down the production. And the one that most impressed me as a student viewer of the film: the shot which follows Chas' bullet into Turner's head before exiting through Borges' shattered image into Powis Square starts with a miniature camera travelling up Pallenberg's vagina.

Jagger has probably the best take on the fog of gossip that surrounds *Performance*: 'those stories are so good I couldn't possibly deny them.' In fact the reality is both more banal and more extraordinary. Banal because many of the more extreme stories like Fox's rumoured real-life crime and the use of Pallenberg's vagina for the hole in Turner's head are simply untrue. Banal because all film sets are the setting for scenes of sex and drugs even if they involve no more than straight affairs and excess alcohol. Extraordinary because it is difficult to think of any studio film since the coming of sound where the production was more out of the control of the studio that paid for it. Extraordinary because Cammell and Roeg used this freedom to improvise with both actors and camera in a manner that can find few Anglo-Saxon parallels outside the very early history of the cinema as Porter and then Griffith developed the language of narrative cinema.

To understand the conditions that allowed Cammell and Roeg, Jagger and Pallenberg, Fox and Shannon to work through the dynamics of the film untroubled by the pompous ministrations of studio execs, it

Preparing to shoot 'Memo from Turner' – arguably the first pop video ever made

is important to recognise the commercial status of the film. The first and most significant fact is that from a financial point of view this film mixed two hot mini-genres, the pop star vehicle and the 'swinging London' film. Cinema's appetite for the stars of popular music goes back to Sinatra and beyond but the coming of the 45 single and the pop charts signalled the birth of a new teen market.

It has taken the studios a long time to work out the premises of the action film and the various other Hollywood genres which have kept teenagers of the 80s and the 90s amused; in the meantime Hollywood found the easiest access to the youth market was to provide vehicles for their music idols. Thus was the endless tedium of the Elvis Presley movie born. In Britain, Cliff Richard and Tommy Steele were rolled out to much the same effect and *Spice World* proves that one can never pronounce the final death of even the most terminally suffering genre.

But genre is simply a theoretical shorthand for audience's expectation of what they are going to see. The pop music vehicle's promise to its audience is nothing more than a view of their pop idol more intimate than that offered by the stage performance or the magazine photo – it is the most minimal of genres, and this provides the basic financial justification for the investment by Warner Bros. and for their nonchalance about what was being produced. The solid commercial asset at the centre of the film was Mick Jagger, the lead singer of the world's second most successful pop group – and provided he was on camera and in focus, that asset was secure.

But the ambitions of Warner Bros. were in fact set higher than what must have been their worst-case bottom-line calculations. The new Seven Arts management who had bought the company from the ageing Jack Warner were busy proving their credentials as a home for creative talent. They also wanted to make a film which would capture the new youth culture and its capital, London. The American studios had proved spectacularly bad at this exercise; *Duffy* had been one of many painful exercises now consigned to the dustbin of history. But there had been a series of films which had got closer: Dick Lester's film with the Beatles, *A Hard Day's Night*, Roman Polanski's *Repulsion* and, above all, Michelangelo Antonioni's *Blowup*. All had shown a foreigner's view of the capital. Now through the agency of an American who lived in London, a Hollywood studio was on the real inside track. A film about swinging London by a swinging Londoner.

It is these contexts which explain what is finally the most extraordinary fact about this extraordinary movie. A Hollywood studio committed a serious budget to a film in which almost all the principals, both cast and crew, were absolute beginners. More than that, Warner Bros. allowed them to shoot entirely on location with no representative of the studio to ensure that they would produce an acceptable movie. This trust was partly the result of the personal relationship between Ken Hyman who, along with his father, owned Seven Arts, the parent company of Warner Bros., and Sandy Lieberson but it was also undoubtedly a sign of the times. *Performance* was shot in the summer and autumn of 1968 following a spring when the youth culture which had been building since the early 60s looked set for a brief instant to change all the known rules. It cannot have been difficult to argue that Cammell and Roeg were using new methods for new times.

Finally, and probably most significantly, *Performance* was produced extremely efficiently. In the end financial control and aesthetic control come down to the same thing in nine cases out of ten. Corporate wisdom would dictate that if the cash flow was under control then so was the film. However, corporate wisdom had reckoned without the decision to use as a line producer David Cammell, Donald's younger brother. While Sandy Lieberson quietened the suits, David Cammell was to ensure that the film stayed on budget and to schedule. So concerned was Donald Cammell to avoid all appearances of nepotism that it was Lieberson and Roeg who approached his brother to ask whether he would 'run' the film with the credit of associate producer. In one way it was an inspired choice, David Cammell at that time owned a commercials company with Hugh Hudson and Robert Brownjohn. Commercials were by the mid-60s the industrial cutting edge of the film business. A commercials producer would not baulk at the vast array of lenses or even the changes of gauge that the directors were contemplating for *Performance*. And Lieberson was particularly taken by the thought of running the film out of the company's offices in Chelsea. But, at the same time, it is difficult to believe that Cammell and Roeg were not influenced by other considerations. Donald's brother would be less likely to mind the improvisations and changes of schedule that the directors must have known would take place in the second half of the film. And if he did mind, he was much less likely to go running to Warner Bros. than a seasoned professional with no loyalty to the director. And David Cammell, whatever his experience in advertising, was anything but a seasoned professional. Thus, to the team of debutantes and novices was added a line producer who had never produced a feature film. By a series of events in which both luck and judgment played a part, the cast and crew of *Performance*, as they started shooting in the week of 29 July 1968, were enjoying a degree of freedom normally only granted to a group of avant-garde enthusiasts working with a mechanically operated 16mm camera and 400 feet of black and white stock. By an even greater stroke of good fortune their inexperience meant that most of them did not realise how lucky they were. Wasn't this how all films were made? And if it wasn't, then wasn't it how all films would be made in the future?

Performance was not by any means the first film to eschew studios for locations, nor to use non-professionals; both of these choices classed it firmly within the European traditions of Italian neo-realism and the French New Wave; improvisation too was part of these European traditions as well as playing a much larger part in Hollywood history than is often allowed. It was the combination of all these features with studio financing and a genuinely stellar cast which makes *Performance* such a unique production.

David Cammell's first task was to find the locations that the directors were demanding. The insistence on location shooting, apart from the bonus of removing oneself from the surveillance of the executives, was that it allowed the camera access to a reality that studios could only simulate but never re-create. Cammell had been friends in Paris with Raoul Coutard, Jean-Luc Godard's cameraman, and it is impossible to know how much Cammell had learnt from him but both Roeg and Cammell seemed to follow a Godardian aesthetic insisting that the initial reality with which the camera is confronted is as authentic as possible. This authenticity is not however an end in itself but the raw material from which the film is then fashioned. If that raw material is produced from a studio in which actors and technicians take their accustomed and easy physical and social places then the material has not enough interest to warrant further work. It is the interaction of people and place on location which allows a spark of life to pass on to celluloid.

The locations were almost all found by David Cammell, who had himself argued strongly to make the film an all-location shoot. As they searched London for a cavernous house to be Turner's domain, he remembered an illegal gambling club in Lowndes Square where he had been thoroughly fleeced in the early 60s. This not only provided the setting for much of the second half of the film (the basement scenes were shot in Hyde Park Gate) but it was here that the sets for Chas' flat were built. Other significant locations were the Royal Garden Hotel in Kensington, which provided Harry Flowers' bedroom, and the top floor of a Chinese restaurant in Wardour Street which housed the gangster's office.

All film productions are beset by difficulties. *Performance* certainly had its share: some familiar, some unique. In the familiar category was the threat delivered to David Cammell amd Sandy Lieberson three weeks into production by their next-door neighbour in Lowndes Square. After informing the startled producer that he should be aware that there were 'more titled people living in Lowndes Square than in any other Square except Eaton Square', the lady went on to complain about the noise and disturbance that the film crew were causing. When it became clear that she meant business and that the film's landlord had broken the terms of his lease in allowing the house to be used for filming, both

David Cammell and Sandy Lieberson were forced to spend some anxious days at the High Court before a solution was found.

But if it is usual on location shooting to find that some locals are less than appreciative of the arrival of a film crew and equipment in their midst, it is less frequent to have the financiers suspend the shoot or a lab threaten to destroy the negative.

Every day executives would turn up to Warner Bros. screening rooms to watch with Sandy Lieberson the previous day's rushes. The story goes that they rarely saw anything, mainly because their lunches had been so good that they were soon fast asleep, particularly as the inexperienced editor insisted on screening all the takes rather than a selection as is usual. The film was shot in sequence, so it wasn't until halfway through the movie that the normally somnolent executives were confronted with Turner sharing his bath with Pherber and Lucy. Sleep was banished as the well-fuelled execs realised that they were watching a film that was going to break every notion of what might or might not be acceptable on a Hollywood screen. The plethora of naked bodies and the simple acceptance of an easygoing polymorphous perversion were not only genuinely shocking but clearly unreleasable.

The script was not being followed, the directors clearly didn't know what they were doing, there was only one solution: abandon the film. And that was the news that an irate Ken Hyman delivered to Sandy Lieberson, the friend he felt had betrayed him. The shoot was indeed suspended over a weekend. Lieberson finally persuaded Warner Bros. to finish the movie, but from now on the studio was to regard the film with the gravest of suspicions as a mistake that they never should have made. It would be wrong to underestimate the extent to which the executives were genuinely shocked by a film that presented sex and violence without any of the veils or the glosses that Hollywood demanded. At the same time it is worth recalling that this was a film which had been given the green light in the spring of 1968, at the high point of the wave of the 60s, and that the bath scene had been shot in September by which time reaction had triumphed in both Paris and Chicago. *Performance* was thus born at the moment of the death of the 60s; it is what makes the film so wonderful for us now, it was what made it so difficult for its makers then.

If the first half of the film follows the approved script closely, the second half abandons almost all but the setting and the characters. When this decision was made and to whom it was communicated is almost impossible to determine. It is certain that Warner Bros. didn't know, but neither it seems did James Fox who would turn up with his memorised script under his arm day after day when it should have been clear to him that the new pages with which the directors arrived had little to do with the script and everything to do with the improvised drama being played out on the set.

It is this improvisation, and its 'edginess' (to use Jagger's term again), which is the real basis for the rumours that surrounded the *Performance* shoot from the beginning of September as they began to film the second half. When one has discounted the more extreme claims of 'Spanish Tony' Sanchez about the drug intake at Lowndes Square[15] and when one is sceptical of those who claim that Cammell was having affairs with all four principal actors, it is still the case that a fair quantity of drugs were consumed and that the sex scenes with Jagger, Pallenberg and Breton were the most explicit ever recorded for a Hollywood picture.

But it is not the sex and drugs which were the real scandal on the set of *Performance*; it was the fact that the performance of the actors ceased to be the representation of a text and became instead the acting out of their fundamental relationships. Fox, himself, has the clearest perception of this as he recollects the filming of nearly thirty years ago. He remembers sitting in the green room while Pallenberg and Jagger played sexually with each other in an attempt, certainly encouraged by Cammell, to break down any distinction between representation and reality. More importantly he recalls Pallenberg's dislike of him as too 'straight' and sees this as crucial to the power of the scenes between them. Pallenberg disclaims such emotions in favour of an account which makes a joke of her continuous promises to spike Fox's drinks with acid. However, the power of her laugh in the film as Chas pathetically clings to his normality makes nonsense of her disclaimer. And, indeed, Pallenberg was the best placed of the actors to understand exactly what was happening; for it was Pallenberg's own excursions into the avant-garde which were, according to Cammell, the initial inspiration for much of this aspect of the film.

The 60s were, in general, the decade in which representation came under attack. Happenings and situations, the breaking down of the divide between actor and audience; this was the currency of the era. Like much else of that period, the intellectual impetuses often stretched back to the Parisian avant-garde of the 20s. In this case the crucial figure is Antonin Artaud whose thought is consciously echoed in *Performance*'s single most famous line, when Turner tells Chas: 'The only performance that makes it, that really makes it, that makes it all the way is the one that achieves madness.'

Artaud's dissatisfaction with the theatre of his day found expression in the elaboration of the theory and theses of the Theatre of Cruelty.[16] These writings imagined a drama in which the artificialities of text and speech had been left behind in favour of a drama of gesture and screams. It is doubtful whether Artaud was ever really proposing an actual strategy for the stage because any one performance which accomplished his aims would also have inaugurated an entirely new cycle of civilisation in which the whole relation between body and spirit would have been transformed. But many of his insights into the relation of theatre to primitive ritual were central to experiments such as those carried out by the Living Theatre in the 60s. Those experiments had enchanted Anita Pallenberg and it is clear that it was through her that these ideas had influenced Cammell.

Artaud was also an indirect influence on both directors. For his work is part of the context of Cocteau's *Blood of a Poet* (1931) which was a key reference point for both Roeg and Cammell. Despite Artaud's considerable career as a screen actor which included Marat in Gance's *Napoleon* (1927) and a part in Dreyer's *Jeanne d'Arc*, he only saw one of his own projects reach the screen, *The Seashell and the Clergyman*, and he disowned this film at its premiere in 1928. However, when Cocteau's film was unveiled four years later, Artaud was to claim that it had stolen its hallucinatory images and elliptical cutting from his own project. Ignoring the charge of direct plagiarism, there is no doubt that Cocteau's 'realistic documentary of unreal events' is in both method and matter close both to Artaud and to *Performance*.

Artaud was to despair finally of the cinema's potential because the cinematic apparatus seemed to split audience from representation so thoroughly that it was impossible for the events on the screen to touch the audience in the fundamental fashion that he demanded. But Artaud had reckoned without the technological advances of the cinema and without the genius of someone like Roeg who was able to take those advances and place them at the service of an aesthetic devoted to understanding a reality which cannot be reduced to a simple question of representation. Roeg's use of lenses, camera position, filters and even of different stock (at some points the film lapses into black and white) and gauges (the threesome in Powis Square was shot in 16mm) means that the viewer is never simply observing the events of the film, for the viewer's vision is part of the action. The climax of this engagement comes at the end of the film where Chas and Turner become one. It is at this point that interpretation cannot avoid relying on drives and identifications that come from the spectator's side of the screen. Vision has so clearly been divorced from knowledge that it is only our own beliefs that guarantee our understanding. The film's inability to interpret what we see for us is foregrounded in the opening sequence of the film in which the black Rolls Royce and Chas' and Dana's lovemaking are intercut in such a way as to leave it completely unclear as to the direct relationship between them. The very first impression is that Chas and Dana are actually inside the Rolls. When it becomes obvious that they are not, the interior of the Rolls becomes a mysterious space hiding one knows not what infamy and perversion. Such visual riddles are the standard fare of Hollywood films and it is the business of such films to produce a narrative which resolves the riddles and leaves the viewer in the clear. *Performance* refuses such solutions and as the Rolls (now white not black) drives away at the end of the film our vision can no more warrant our knowledge of what it contains than it could at the beginning. If we know the car's contents it is because of the journey we have taken with the film, the performance that we have been obliged and delighted to undertake.

The first historic surge of realism is always an emphasis on what is being represented; the delight in the power of representation; the moment of a Balzac or a Rossellini and the laying out of society as spectacle. The even more potent mimesis is when the representation itself is understood as essential to the reality it depicts: the moment of Joyce or Godard when turn-of-the-century Dublin or 60s Paris includes *Ulysses* or *À bout de souffle* as part of their very definition. Now we are no longer spectators but participants. Cammell's and Roeg's movie reproduces London in 1968; it makes us part of that metropolis, a reality that it promises for us each time it unwinds.

And one aspect of that reality is sex presented in ways that are unprecedented in mainstream cinema. Cammell wanted to get the viewer under the sheets in an intimacy which the camera had never before attempted. Roeg realised that the only way to achieve the effect was to abandon the 35mm camera and to use a wind-up 16mm Bolex. And so as Jagger, Pallenberg and Breton busied themselves in the huge double bed, they were accompanied by Cammell on one side and Roeg plus Bolex on the other. Roeg claims to this day that he can still see Donald's face lifting the sheets and asking 'How was it for you?'

The rushes from that day went off to the studio as usual although not before the clapper loader had warned David Cammell that he expected trouble. Sure enough David Cammell received a call from Humphrey's, the film's lab, very early in the morning saying that the previous day's film contravened the obscenity laws and that the lab were going to destroy it forthwith. After a hastily arranged meeting and much negotiation, Sandy Lieberson and David Cammell managed to retrieve the negative but they were then obliged to sit and watch as the chief executive of the lab destroyed the print with a hammer and chisel.

And so legends are born. It is true that Keith Richards patrolled the streets outside Lowndes Square ferrying Anita to and from a shoot that he despised. It is true that Robert Fraser who had let his flat to Anita Pallenberg for the duration of the production then refused to move out and that each night Richards and Fraser would pore scorn on the efforts of the film-makers. It is true that Fraser was finally banned from the set although nobody can remember the specific offence. And so on and so forth. None of this would be of the slightest interest were it not for the fact that the method of film-making caught and refracted every tension and nuance that played across the cast. It is the method that is crucial to understand and it was a method that required genuine discipline. The furore at Humphrey's was not allowed to disrupt film or schedule and processing was simply transferred to Technicolor. *Performance* came in on or about both schedule and budget. The shoot that was famous for its indulgence and excess had in fact been conducted with extraordinary rigour and dedication.

THE EDIT

. . . .

Editing is the fundamental principle of almost all cinema to date. Avant-garde film-makers like Michael Snow may experiment with the possibilities offered within one take, but brilliant as such experiments are they remain marginal to the cinema that we know, a cinema based on the juxtaposition of images that are fundamentally incongruous. The whole development of classical Hollywood cinema is to exploit and conceal the possibilities of editing; to motivate the movement from image to image in terms either of narrative or psychology, moving seamlessly between objective and subjective points of view so that the spectator never confronts the problematics of vision; the questions of the relation between vision and knowledge; vision and belief. *Performance* does not refuse these classical rules but it continuously cuts to other rhythms which suggest new connections between vision and knowledge; that what we get is far more complicated than what we see.

This extraordinarily complex editing style is divided into two different periods by the exigencies of what was becoming a legendarily difficult studio production. The first stage was in London after the shoot had finished. The first editor, who had screened the rushes at such length, was replaced by Antony Gibbs whose credits included *Taste of Honey* (1961), *Loneliness of the Long Distance Runner* (1962) and *Tom Jones* (1963). The film was now beset by continuous studio opposition and it was nearly a year before Cammell, Roeg and Lieberson presented their cut to Warner Bros. Warners were outraged. It was not simply that they objected to the sex and violence, which they did, but they were outraged that a pop star vehicle did not produce the pop star until over halfway through the movie. If Jagger was the fundamental economic asset, then it was an asset which was buried in an opening which contained a great deal of violent crime but not a hint of Jagger. They might not have noticed this detail in the script but they certainly noticed it in the finished film. To compound their outrage the second half of the film bore little relation to the script they had funded. Instead of a dramatic bust, there were endless mind and sex games.

We do not have a copy of this cut, which seems to have been finished about a year after the shoot in autumn 1969, but we do possess a transcript which reveals a very different film than the one we know. The first half of the film is much longer and the various elements of Chas' story are told in linear fashion. The differences can be emphasised by noting that in this first cut there are only two edits juxtaposing the black Rolls Royce and Chas and Dana engaged in violent narcissistic sex; in the finished film there are over fifty cuts between bodies and vehicle.

For Roeg and Lieberson the news that Warner Bros. would not accept the cut and that the studio wanted the editing to move to Los Angeles was disastrous. Roeg's *Walkabout* was now ready to go and he could no longer delay his departure for Australia; Lieberson too was set to make *Mary Queen of Scots* with Sandy Mackendrick. In any case *Performance* now seemed doomed. Moving the editing back to Los Angeles was a standard ploy; it simply meant that the studio would now control everything. What lay ahead were endless battles and a butchered film. The three set out for Los Angeles and agreed the principles of the new edit but Roeg and Lieberson then left for their new projects. Initially Warner's post-production supervisor Rudy Fehr assigned Cammell a totally unsympathetic editor. But he soon tracked down a new collaborator: Frank Mazzola. In Mazzola, Cammell found a partner as sympathetic as Roeg; an editor who knew the rules backwards but knew them well enough to abandon them whenever necessary. Cammell was to work with Mazzola for the rest of his career. The foundation of that partnership came in the six months (from the end of 1969 to the middle of 1970) when they worked on *Performance*.

Mazzola was pure Los Angeles. The child of vaudeville actors whose father had been the first contract player at Fox, Mazzola had grown up with the 50s gangs of LA. He started work as an actor in the early 50s and was cast for a minor role in *Rebel without a Cause*. Nick Ray had appointed him director of authenticity for James Dean and so close did the three of them become in the course of the shooting that they planned to start a production company together before Dean's death. When Cammell met him he was an editor of thirteen years' standing in Hollywood but he was also of the American generation which had been transfixed by European cinema of the 60s and particularly the French New Wave. Perhaps most important of all a deep devotion to jazz inclined him towards an improvisatory aesthetic.

In later years Cammell was to give all the credit for *Performance*'s 'innovative montage' to Mazzola. Mazzola himself, however, only claims credit for the first half of the film and emphasises Cammell's own role in the process. Cammell and Roeg had been given a clear brief from

It was the violence of this scene that most appalled the studio

Warner Bros. to shorten the film's first half so that the viewers got to
Jagger quickly and to cut down on the sex and violence. Cammell and
Roeg did decide to leave out some of the more shocking violence,
particularly from the scene in which Chas is beaten by Joey Maddox, but
they had decided on a strategy of very fast cuts. The speed of some of
the cuts now meant that there was technically less sex or violence on
screen, but their impact was, if anything, intensified. But in shortening
the first half Cammell got the chance to explore editorial techniques
which he and Roeg had already attempted in London but which they had
not fully developed.

WIlliam Burroughs was a figure Cammell had come across both in
Chelsea and Morocco (there is a direct reference to him in the film when
Pherber wonders whether they shouldn't call Dr Burroughs to deal with
Chas). Burroughs had spent much of the 60s developing his cut-up
techniques in which material (be it text, tape or film) was cut up and
recombined at random. The aim of the procedure was to discover
connections and parallels which the conscious mind, too mired in the
world of meaning, was not able to see. The cut-ups could provide access

to levels of textual significance that escaped more conscious manipulation. This technique was also close to the methods used in Kenneth Anger's *Scorpio Rising* which was another key reference point for Cammell. With Mazzola in Los Angeles Cammell was able to improvise in the edit as he had on the shoot. The film we know began to fall into place.

The final major creative element of the film was also provided in Los Angeles when Jack Nitzsche agreed to compose and arrange the soundtrack. Nitzsche was already a legendary figure in the pop world, a classically trained musician who had worked through every stage of recent history, producing and arranging for Phil Spector, Sonny Bono and the Rolling Stones. And it was the Stones, and Keith Richards in particular, who guided Nitzsche towards *Performance*. Nitzsche had been asked to produce a soundtrack for the film *Candy* but his work had been rejected. When he played it to Keith Richards, Keith was impressed and suggested that he do the music for *Performance*. Much of this, such as the proto-rap band the Last Poets and Jagger's 'Memo for Turner', was in place. But Nitzsche was to add not only a strong blues score but also a new kind of instrument: an electronic synthesizer. So new in fact that none had yet been produced, but Nitszche's contacts enabled him to get hold of a prototype which was used at the recording session. So crucial are the synthesizer's pulses to the rhythm of the film that it is difficult to imagine *Performance* without them but, like the very fast editing, they only exist because of the studio's initial resistance to the film.

Not that the resistance was diminishing. At a test screening in Santa Monica in March 1970 one executive's wife vomited with shock. So vocal was the audience in its displeasure that the film had to be stopped and the paying customers offered their money back. If that was not enough, Lieberson and Roeg were not happy with what Cammell had done. Lieberson still feels the London cut was the more balanced film. Roeg had to be persuaded by Cammell not to take his name off the picture. In a late interview Cammell suggests that Roeg was unhappy with the final edit but Roeg insists that his unhappiness was entirely to do with the sound mix and he did succeed in his argument that the film should be redubbed to get a better sound balance. Finally Roeg pronounced himself happy. Now all that was needed was for Warner Bros. to release it.

THE RELEASE

. . . .

Performance's travails had coincided with a change of ownership at Warner Bros. Seven Arts sold the company to Kinney, a company whose core business was car parking. Without this change of ownership *Performance* would never have been released. Ken Hyman had made the decision to abandon the film which he was convinced would be a commercial disaster as well as a moral outrage. There were even rumours that he had attempted to bury the negative so as to be finally released from coping with this troublesome movie. The new studio head was John Calley and he took a different attitude and promised to release the cut that Cammell and Mazzola had prepared.

There was, however, one more hurdle before the film finally was released in the United States in the summer of 1970. Warner's president, Ted Ashley, saw the film and was so appalled that he ordered fresh cuts. Cammell desperately tried to garner support for the film, eliciting telegrams of support from Kenneth Anger and David Maysles, writing to Stanley Kubrick and composing a telegram to Ashley which he signed with Mick Jagger. The telegram informs the president of Warner Bros. that *Performance* is about 'the perverted love affair between Homo Sapiens and Lady Violence' and adds that 'if *Performance* does not upset audiences then it is nothing'.

Finally Warner Bros. agreed to release the film but the choice of date in the first dead week of August hardly implies that the studio was throwing much of its muscle behind it. Indeed as a member of the MPAA, the studio must have been extremely embarrassed at releasing an X-rated film and must have both hoped and planned that the film would have as limited a release as possible. The poster, and the ads based on it, was, however, magnificent. At the top of the poster in huge letters was the simple legend: 'Vice. And Versa.' Beneath this were juxtaposed photos of Fox and Jagger showing Jagger first as feminine and then as masculine while Fox alternated in the reverse order. The catch line was simple: 'This film is about madness. And sanity. Fantasy. And reality. Death. And life. Vice. And versa.' The mainstream critics loathed the film. Their reviews, particularly, as I noted earlier, those of John Simon in the *New York Times* and Richard Schickel in *Time*, castigated the film at every level from incompetence to immorality. The virulence of tone and the levels of aggression bear witness to the fact that *Performance* was an unusually powerful movie. If upsetting audiences was the criterion of success then *Performance* was a major hit. By most other criteria, it was a failure. Despite some very good reviews (Simon's piece in the *New York Times* was a response to a favourable review by Peter Schjeldahl),[17] the film died quickly. It is doubtful whether *Performance* was ever likely to be a major success in America given its setting in a foreign capital but what chances it had were destroyed by the date of the release, the reaction of the mainstream critics and by Warner's decision to dub Harry Flowers' voice. It is difficult to understand this decision because, while Amercans find many English dialects notoriously difficult to understand, cockney makes an easier transatlantic crossing than most. Johnny Shannon's voice is one of the centres of the film, providing a power and momentum which bind narrative and image together. The weak and badly dubbed voice Warner Bros. provided him with deprives the first half of the film of much of its menace and attraction.

But the release that really mattered was in London and that came in January 1971 with a charity premiere for the drugs organisation Release. Release rang up Tony Elliott the owner of *Time Out* to enlist his support and once Elliott had seen it, he threw the entire weight of the magazine behind the film. Not only did Jagger grace the cover of the regular magazine but *Time Out* produced a special supplement/poster which accorded the film the status of an instant classic. The underground press, so crucial to the London of the late 60s, had found their film. The reviews were excellent and the box-office good. Perhaps more important, and this I can testify to personally, *Time Out*'s judgment was immediately confirmed by young Londoners across the capital. It is this generation, thirty years on and in the aftermath of Cammell's death, who continue to press its claims in a flurry of media activity of which this book is a part.

AFTERMATH

. . . .

It is a curious irony that by the time *Performance* achieved its success most of its creators wanted little to do with it. James Fox had abandoned acting to follow a Christian vocation and was not to see the film for another eight years. Mick Jagger had not enjoyed the experience of his next film, *Ned Kelly* (1970), and his interviews at the time indicate little of the interest in film or ideas that had animated his original engagement. Both Pallenberg and Breton were too involved with heroin addiction to be much concerned with a film from what was, by now, their long distant past. Johnny Shannon was perhaps the most contented member of the cast. If the second half of the film had passed him by at the premiere, the first half had established him as an actor for British cinema and television and it was as an actor that he would work for the next thirty years. Sandy Lieberson felt himself dogged by a film which had been three years in the making and which was never going to make any money. However proud he was of the movie he wanted to move on to projects which involved fewer headaches and more profits. Even Roeg's feelings seem to have been mixed. At the height of the arguments with Warner Bros.

Frank Mazzola and Donald Cammell in 1995

they had threatened to sue him for professional negligence. Although he too was proud of the film, its post-production had been a nightmare. He had now embarked on a successful directing career in which *Performance* simply looked like a prelude to his solo efforts which would include *Don't Look Now* (1973) and *Bad Timing* (1980) among many others. The only figure who seemed unequivocally delighted was Donald Cammell. He could hardly have thought, as he savoured the success of *Performance* in London in January 1971, that it would be six years before he made another film (*Demon Seed* with Julie Christie), a further decade before he would make the low-budget *White of the Eye*, and a decade more before Nu Image would butcher his film *Wild Side* so badly that he would take his name off the credits shortly before he shot himself in the head in April 1996.

Cammell's life in Los Angeles over the next three decades is, rather like the story of *Performance*, the stuff of legend. The sexual excess, the continuous fights with studios, the multiple failed projects with Marlon Brando: there is material there for several memoirs, a whole series of novels and, almost inevitably, a bio-pic. But whatever story is told it is difficult to believe that *Performance* will not hold pride of place: the one moment when ambition and execution came together, when personal obsession engaged with social movement, when avant-garde could be conjugated with mainstream.

Performance's own afterlife has been relatively curious. It was greeted by almost all the British reviewers as an instant classic, one of those films whose greatness is immediately apparent and the writings that followed Cammell's death made clear that it had retained that status for many. It is also the case that the writing on *Performance* from early reviews by Gavin Millar and Tom Milne to more recent articles by Peter Wollen and Jon Savage has been of the very highest order. However, it is not a film that has commended itself to academic film historians and theorists. This is not surprising. A film which stands for a decade in which politics and pleasure were inseparably linked, *Performance* was never going to recommend itself to the political orthodoxies of the puritanical 70s or the hedonist 80s. A film which could stress the fundamental centrality of homosexuality but as a component of heterosexuality; which made a film about the impact of black culture on London but featured only one minor black character;[18] which could look to the working class for liberation but ignore politics: *Performance* was

Narcissism at work: Chas observes his own performance

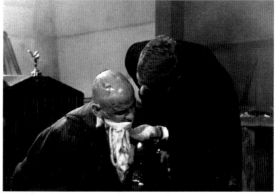

Chas addresses his remarks to the lawyer – by destroying his car and shaving his chauffeur's head; Harry Flowers and Dennis

'I am a bullet': Chas kills Joey Maddocks

Chas changes route from Barnstaple to Powis square

'Here's to old England': Turner as Flowers

Death and rebirth

Chas shoots Turner; the bullet exits to Powis Square, smashing the image of Borges; the final merger

not made with the politically correct in mind. And on one front, gender, it probably deserves the critique it invites. The proud independence which Pallenberg brings to Pherber reproduces her own relation to Cammell and the film. Michèle Breton, however, proved a casualty of the liberated 60s disappearing into poverty and addiction and it would be easy to make a case for Cammell manipulating both women into figuring in the ideal fantasy of the male voyeur.

If the complexity of its figuring of sexuality, class and race were not enough of a deterrent to the ambitious film scholar, *Performance* is a film which demands a very wide range of cultural reference for its interpretation. The knowledges needed to write the book on *Performance* and painting, on *Performance* and music, on *Performance* and literature, on *Performance* and London are not knowledges encouraged by the current division of the faculties in the university. Whether *Performance* will have the strength of a genuine classic and produce the scholars it requires or whether it will remain as a historical footnote, a cult film for *soixante-huitards*, is something on which I am inevitably unable to make a final judgment. What is certain is that the film performs its time, gives voice to the sounds and meanings of its moment, articulates a Utopian vision. *Performance*'s future is not simply an academic judgment on a text, it will be tied to the whole legacy of a generation which bought its counter-culture from record stores, drug dealers and chemists; exchanges for which the full reckoning has yet to be calculated.

CODA: POLITICS AND MAGIC

'L'eroticisme il est possible de dire qu'il est l'approbation de la vie jusque dans la mort.' The opening line of Georges Bataille's *L'eroticisme* weakly rendered into English as, 'Eroticism, it is possible to say, is the affirmation of life even into death itself,'[19] could well figure as the most appropriate epigram for *Performance*. That Cammell read him in Paris is certain, but then Bataille's work, which in its eclectic merging of medieval scholarship, anthropology, economics, Marxism and pornography defies all classification, was part of the obliged reading of the Parisian 60s. What is less certain is whether Cammell had read Bataille widely enough to have fully grasped his use of modern anthropology as a tool to find a new balance between sacred and profane in the contemporary world. But Bataille's emphasis on death and expenditure as the culminating moments of life and production makes his work the best guide to the thematics of *Performance*. Above all, Bataille argues that any new revolutionary social order requires the acceptance that the culmination of the most life-giving and social drives is death and destruction whether one regards those drives from the point of view of the individual or the collectivity.

For Bataille the fundamental drives of the body find their most powerful representation in a recurrent fantasy in which the inside and outside of the body are ruptured by a hole. This hole whose two most localised representatives are the anus and the eye achieves fantasmatic climax when anus and eye are joined together in a huge erection of energy which literally blasts the skull off.[20] Whether the hole which runs as a motif through *Performance* is a direct reference to Bataille or whether Cammell and Roeg were simply working with the same series of fundamental fantasies is unimportant in this context. What is certain is that Turner's explanation, 'The blood of this vegetable is boring a hole. This second hole is penetrating the hole of your face. The skull of your bone,' takes up previous references in the film and prepares us for the explosive penetration of the final scene. To understand death as an affirmation of life is the effort of Bataille's thought, it is also the effort of *Performance*.

There is a simple symbolic journey at the heart of *Performance* which takes Chas from the narcissistic repressed homosexuality of the opening sequence to the open liberated sexuality of the final minutes of the film. The opening sequence shows us a soulless display of sexual pyrotechnics as Chas and Dana engage in modern sex complete with all the necessary aids: whips and mirrors. The Randy Newman song which accompanies this scene, 'Gone Dead Train', emphasises that we are looking at the very death of desire: 'the fire in my boiler up and quit before I came.' The image which freezes, in every sense of the word, this coupling has Chas regarding a mirror as Dana services him orally: her actions simply the confirming moment of his potency. Lacan in one of his more memorable aphorisms declared that 'Man comes because of his own organ, Woman comes because of the other'.[21] Chas' sexuality is focused fetishistically on his own maleness in the way which Freud suggested in one of his most radical essays is the prototype for all masculinity.[22] But that sexuality is broken open by the mirror that Pherber manipulates in her encounter with Chas and which projects a female face and body on to the surface of Chas' masculinised body. It is this acceptance of the trauma of difference, the recognition of the body's interchangeability, that enables Chas both to embrace Turner and to make love to the boyish Lucy. This passage of sexual initiation is clearly meant to transform Chas completely and a great deal of the power of the film relies on the very brief scenes between Lucy and Chas after they have made love. It is a testament to the power of Fox's performance that he does convey, in the few lines of dialogue that follow his *Walpurgisnacht*, a complete metamorphosis. This is a Chas not only comfortable in his own skin but able to open himself to the foreign and the other. The repressed homosexuality which underpins the hatred of all difference of gender and race is opened out on to a genuine curiosity about the other: both carnal and spiritual.

That these short scenes are central to the film is borne out by Cammell's and Roeg's desire to re-shoot them a year after the production finished. Cammell wrote to Lieberson on 25 August 1969 to say that they wanted to emphasise 'the genuine moment of tenderness and compassion between these two that is the whole point of the scene'. The shot the directors wanted was a close-up of Lucy on the bed with Chas backlit in the foreground, but even without this punctuation the scenes carry their necessary charge.

But this is not the end of the story, even if an orthodox Freudian might wish to call a halt here. There is still the cataclysmic final confrontation between Chas and Turner, their ultimate alliance which Cammell had not foreseen in any of the pre-shoot scripts but without which the film would not achieve its genuine catharsis. There are, in the very logic of the film, a host of interpretations for these last minutes. Two, however, are among the most insistent. The first, pessimistic, would stress the impossibility of the ego to surrender its narcissistic defences. Whatever initial release there is will be followed by an overwhelming counter-reaction – a chilling upsurge of violence as the fetishistic identifications lock back in place. Chas kills Turner because he cannot bear the force of the drives that the singer has made him acknowledge. Thanatos, god of death, triumphs over Eros, god of love. A more optimistic reading would have Chas' violent passage into Turner's body as the inevitable result of the gangster's opening to the possibilities of his being. Chas and Turner literally merge as both fully take on the identity of the other. Here Eros triumphs over Thanatos at the price of acknowledging Thanatos' supremacy.

To use this Freudian vocabulary is already to risk reducing *Performance* to an interpretative schema whereby the film represents a separate realm of sexuality. But the whole emphasis of the film is to banish representation in favour of performance, a performance in which the spectator is a key actor. The rejection of representation is not only the key to much of the 60s aesthetics but it is also at the core of the most innovative political movement of that decade: situationism. From street riots of enrages in Strasbourg and Paris to genteel meetings of philosophers in Oxford may seem an impossibly long distance but performance is also the key term for the most important philosophy of the decade.[23] J. L. Austin's *How to Do Things with Words* (the title itself suggests a magical rather than a philosophical text) is a sustained attempt to break with notions of language as representation in favour of an understanding of language in performance. Austin's theories are not without their precursors; both the later Wittgenstein and the American pragmatists grounded their theories of language in a community of practice, but it is Austin who emphasises again and again that language cannot be understood outside its role in very specific social situations. That his definition of those situations is extraordinarily prim and parochial and that he explicitly tries to distance his theories from all questions of theatricality should not obscure how close he is to the political and aesthetic avant-garde of the decade.[24]

Austin, beneath his conservative exterior, is perhaps the most radical of those philosophers who question any notion of an interior

Destruction and discovery: games with mirrors

essence which acts as the ground or foundation of action and intention. For Austin we are our performances and Cammell's and Roeg's film can be seen as a rehearsal of this philosophical argument in the field of sexuality.

Why *Performance* remains such a crucial film is that it gathers up these themes – aesthetic, political, philosophical and sexual – which still dominate our intellectual and emotional lives. We live in the wake of the 60s. To take an example almost at random, Judith Butler's fascinating theses on sexuality and performativity often read like extended, if unintended, commentaries on Cammell's and Roeg's film.[25]

There seems to me no final way to legislate for interpretations at the end of *Performance*. The camera's penetration of Turner's body, its shattering of Borges' image and its transgression of every rule of spatial construction mean that the final eerie minutes of the film are entirely our invention. Much as Chas re-runs early moments from a conversation with Harry Flowers to produce a vastly different office party as Turner dictates his memo, so the ending allows us to sample and select from the film to produce our pattern. Of course, this infinity of interpretations is a feature of any complex text; what marks out *Performance* is that it is one of the very few genuinely modernist texts of the cinema (Godard provides most of the others) where that infinity of interpretation is foregrounded.

Even given the film's paradoxical ending which multiplies interpretations exponentially, it is possible to insist on the importance of a political reading of *Performance*. Neither Cammell nor Roeg were men with a great deal of interest in the political. Cammell, in particular, seems deliberately to have eschewed it. If he seems to have read incredibly widely in the Parisian texts of the 60s, his reading avoided Althusser and all the Maoisant posturings of the time. Deborah Dixon remembers flying out of Paris to join *Performance*'s pre-production on the last flight before the May events closed the country in a general strike but she does not remember Cammell asking any questions about the May events or ever showing any interest in politics.

But *Performance*'s politics have nothing to do with the epi-phenomena of parties and governments and everything to do with the realities of class exploitation. England is represented as a country enthralled to a vicious and cynical ruling class. The lawyer and the gangster are, despite differences of language and social class, ultimately united in their common exploitation of a people only glimpsed on streets and offices, punters whose faces merge from the jury room to the pornographic cinema. The only area which lies outside this control is the house at 81 Powis Square, the locus of the sex and drugs and music which has the potential to transform the society. But Turner is an intellectual has-been; a man whose daemon has left him until Chas appears at his door.

Fredric Jameson reinvented the Marxist hermeneutic in his *Political Unconscious* by seeking the fundamental social level of any text in its unconscious fantasmatic projections of social relations.[26] The politics of a text is not to be measured by its explicit political positions nor by its representation of the class struggle but by the Utopian fantasies which inform its narrative. *Performance* is almost a classic example of such a fantasy. The final fusion of Chas and Turner brings together the two elements in English society which have the power and the energy to transform 'old England'. As East End hood and fading rock star merge in a genuine union which makes a mockery of all the film's sordid alliances, we enter into another realm of social possibility. As Rosey clears up in the house, we discover Turner's body lying in the cupboard where all the picture frames have been stacked: the exterior support may have been discarded but the painting that is Turner is elsewhere. The majority of commentators on *Performance* have Chas being driven off to be killed by Flowers' henchmen but if one follows the logic just sketched then the white Rolls Royce is bound for unimaginable social utopias. It must have been this thought which made Cammell write a second letter to Lieberson pleading for another re-shoot:

> The final shot of 'Performance' is of the greatest importance. It 'generalises' the whole story; in other words, it indicates that the film has moved, during its course, from a purely realistic level to a purely allegorical level.
>
> We see Chas, from the back, get into Harry Flowers' white Rolls-Royce, Harry says, genially, 'Hullo, Chas!' The Rolls moves off. As it passes close to camera, the figure inside in the red wig looks out of the window. The face is Turner's.
>
> Cut to a close high-angle shot, looking down on a street from a building. The white Rolls-Royce comes into close shot (angle down on its roof). As it rolls up the street, we zoom out to

show Central Park West. We continue to pull up and back as the Rolls turns into Central Park. It recedes across the park – a greyish, misty shot. As the camera angles up to follow the car, the New York skyline (of Fifth Avenue in the distance) comes into frame.

The white Rolls recedes across the Park.

End.

… Once more I can't stress enough that Nico's notion to substitute New York – Central Park for Hyde Park (as in the original script) really adds something, on every level, to the last shot of *Performance* that we must make the maximum effort to secure.

America has functioned throughout the film as the Promised Land ('Chin up, uncle! The land of opportunity awaits'); Chas/Turner has come into his Kingdom, reached the Persia of his imagination. The fact that the final moment of liberation breaks national boundaries is no surprise in the film: England and Englishness are finished within the world of *Performance*; frozen in a variety of social and personal fetishes.

The second coming – Chas/Turner slouches towards Bethlehem

Turner's cosmopolitanism needs to break out of the house into the street but he lacks the energy which only Chas can give him.

The fantasy of the union of Turner and Chas, of pop music and violent crime, is also the fantasy of the fundamental unity of the human. The fantasy that each man is all men, that at moments of extreme crisis, particularly sexual crisis, we are all Everyman, is a recurring element in much mystical and magical thinking. It is lent literary authority in the figure of Jorge Luis Borges who is the most insistent reference in the film. It is Borges who provides Rosebloom's reading matter throughout the narrative, it is Borges' most famous story 'El Sur' which is read by Turner to Chas; it is Borges whose image appears at the very limits of the intelligible in the recesses of Turner's skull.

It would be easy to criticise this reading of *Performance* as political allegory. A 70s Marxist would deride the lack of any appeal to an organised working class. Indeed the film portrays the working class as irredeemably stuck; caught in a vicious circle where homosexuality and chauvinism follow each other in frozen narcissisms. Chas' liberation requires the intervention of the middle class, the foreign and the mad. A similar critique could begin from the side of the casting: it would be easy to sneer at a film which placed its hopes for liberation in a James Fox who was to become a committed Christian or a Mick Jagger who would join the liberal decadent wing of the British aristocracy. But all these sneers and derision would miss the fundamental point which is that *Performance* is a genuine sketch of the possibilities of liberation in England in 1968. If the working class is discounted in all but its fundamental energy, it is well to remember Oscar Wilde's quote that he was a socialist not because he loved the working class but because he hated it. If Fox turned to religion and Jagger to the aristocracy, it may be important to reflect on how the counter-culture never fully articulated the relation between spirituality and style, despite the fact that this was its most important promise.

If we accept that we are still living through the failures as well as the successes of the 60s then *Performance* is a key text to which to return again and again to better understand our situation now. Any knowing political criticism of the film presumes a certainty about social relations which the film continually questions. If we want to understand the possibilities of liberation in Britain in the 90s *Performance* remains as rich a text as it did in the 60s. For some the attempt to read *Performance* as political allegory may seem forced, a desperate attempt to yoke the sublime to the ridiculous. But it must be remembered that the political has the possibilities of the sublime even though its realities are all too often ridiculous. In the run-up to *Performance* Jagger was courted by Tom Driberg, the former chairman of the Labour Party, to stand for Parliament.[27] Early in their careers the Kray twins were expelled from the Bethnal Green Conservative Party for violence.[28] If *Performance* sketches the tragic impasses of British life, political history provides a farcical gloss – a ludicrous might have been.

Cammell was not interested in politics but he was interested in magic. Testimony veers widely in this area: many who knew him well say that he had no interest in magic; others claim that it was a constant preoccupation (at the end of his life he said to a close friend, 'I wish I'd never got involved in magic. It fucked everything up'). What is clear is that magic is the hidden underside of modernism. We have to go back to Yeats to find a moment when magic and the cultural transformation of society are clearly articulated together but this link is one of the dominant notes of the twentieth century. It is significant that the key literary references for the film – Bataille and Artaud and Borges and Burroughs – combine, in different forms, a fascination with the esoteric. Indeed one of the tasks that *Performance* urges on us the viewer is a re-reading of the history of the modernism of the 20s in which the link between politics and culture would be reconsidered and that the fights around surrealism (both Bataille and Artaud were expelled from the surrealist movement by the loathsome Leninist Breton) would be more fully explored. Magic would be a key term of this reconsideration. It is impossible to pre-empt the results of such a considerable historical inquiry. It is, however, clear that magic combines a fundamental desire to bring knowledge and being into direct correlation together with a fundamental fear that knowledge will be contaminated by the social. *Performance* might be thought to balance on this knife edge: a genuine act of magic.

NOTES

. . . .

1 Richard Schickel, *Time*, 24 August 1970, p. 61.

2 John Simon, *New York Times*, 23 August 1970.

3 Peter Wollen, *Sight and Sound*, vol. 5 no. 9, September 1995.

4 Jon Savage, *Sight and Sound*, vol. 3 no. 5, May 1993.

5 Nik Cohn, *Today There Are No Gentlemen* (London: Weidenfeld & Nicolson, 1971), p. 55.

6 Marianne Faithfull, *Faithfull* (London: Michael Joseph, 1994), p. 211.

7 *Monthly Film Bulletin*, vol. 35 no. 418, November 1968, pp. 178–9.

8 The full details of this incident involve too many living performers for me to desire to achieve complete accuracy.

9 If one was following this logic automatically one might want to make a case for Jimmy Evans as author, for this murderer was the specific model for Chas. But Evans' story has none of the enabling inclusiveness that characterises Litvinoff's life. See *Respect: Autobiography of Freddie Foreman – Managing Director of British Crime* (London: Century, 1996).

10 It is to Mojo that Turner delivers what could have become an immortal line of 60s kitsch as he explains why he cannot work that day: 'Listen, baby. I've got an orgy on.'

11 Philip Norman's *The Stones* provides a thorough account, *Faithfull* a more personal view.

12 The best book on the Krays remains John Pearson's *The Profession of Violence*.

13 There had of course been numerous attempts at more realistic representations of the northern working class both in such films as *This Sporting Life* and on television in a series like *Z Cars*. But working-class London remains *terra incognita* for most television and film in the 60s.

14 Faithfull, *Faithfull*, pp. 79–80.

15 Antonin 'Spanish Tony' Sanchez was the Stones' drug dealer.

16 Antonin Artaud, *The Theatre and its Double* (London: Calder & Boyars, 1970).

17 *New York Times*, 16 August 1970.

18 The lyrics of 'Wake up Niggers' are the most explicit link between black liberation and the other liberations that the film explores, but the very geography of Powis Square – at the centre of Notting Hill, London's first black neighbourhood – indicates the importance of this racial theme. Wollen's article (*Sight and Sound*, September 1995) is particularly good on the significance of the geography of London in *Performance*.

19 Georges Bataille, *L'eroticisme* (Paris: Editions de Minuit, 1957), p. 17.

20 Bataille, 'The Jesuve' and 'The Pineal Eye', in Allan Stoekl (ed.), *Visions of Excess* (Minnesota: University of Minnesota Press, 1985), pp. 73–90.

21 Jacques Lacan, *Le Seminaire XX: encore* (Paris: Editions du Seuil, 1975), p. 70.

22 Sigmund Freud, 'Fetishism', in *The Complete Psychological Works of Sigmund Freud* (London: The Hogarth Press, 1961), vol. 21, pp. 152–7.

23 Austin's William James' lectures at Harvard which form the basis of *How to Do Things with Words* were delivered in 1955. But the book itself was not published until 1962 and John Searle's influential *Speech Acts* not until seven years later at the end of the decade.

24 It is Derrida who has argued most forcefully that Austin's examples cannot sustain a strong differentiation between ordinary and theatrical uses of language. See 'Signature evenement contexte', in *La Dissemination* (Paris: Editions du Seuil, 1972), pp. 157–83 and the subsequent exchange with Searle: John Searle, 'Reiterating Differences', *Glyph*, vol. 2, 1977, pp. 198–208 and Jacques Derrida, 'Limited Inc. abc', *Glyph*, vol. 2, 1977, pp. 162–254.

25 Judith Butler, *Gender Trouble: Feminism and the Subversion of Identity* (New York and London: Routledge, 1990) and *Bodies That Matter: On the Discursive Limits of 'Sex'* (New York and London: Routledge, 1993). It cannot be too long either before somebody recognises *Performance* as the first 'queer' film.

26 Fredric Jameson, *The Political Unconscious* (Ithaca: Cornell University Press, 1981), pp. 17–103.

27 Faithfull, *Faithfull*, pp. 207–10.

28 Iain Sinclair, *Lights Out for the Territory* (London: Granta, 1997), p. 72.

CREDITS

· ·

Performance

UK
1970

Production Companies
Warner Bros. Inc
A Goodtimes Enterprises
production
Producer
Sanford Lieberson
Associate Producer
David Cammell
Production Manager
Robert Lynn
Unit Manager
Kevin Kavanagh
Directors
Donald Cammell, Nicolas
Roeg
Assistant Director
Richard Burge
Continuity
Anabelle Davis-Goff
Screenplay
Donald Cammell
Director of Photography
Nicolas Roeg
Camera Operator
Mike Molloy
Editors
Antony Gibbs, Brian
Smedley-Aston
Art Director
John Clark
Set Dresser
Peter Young
**Design Consultant for
Turner's House**
Christopher Gibbs
Costume Consultant
Deborah Dixon
Wardrobe
Emma Porteous, Billy Jay
Make-up
Paul Rabiger, Linda De
Vetta
Hairdresser
Helen Lennox

Music
Jack Nitzsche
Music Conductor
Randy Newman
Music Performed by
Ry Cooder, Bobby West,
Russel Titelman, The Merry
Clayton Singers, Milt
Holland, Amiya Dasgupta,
Lowell George, Gene
Parsons
Moog Synthesizer
Bernard Krause
Santur
Nasser Rastigar-Nejad
Songs
'Poor White Hound Dog',
'Performance' by Jack
Nitzsche, performed by
Merry Clayton; 'Turner's
Murder' by Jack Nitzsche,
performed by The Merry
Clayton Singers; 'Dyed,
Dead, Red' by Jack
Nitzsche, performed by
Buffy Saint-Marie; 'Wake
Up Nigger' by Jack
Nitzsche, performed by The
Last Poets; 'Gone Dead
Train' by Jack Nitzsche,
Russel Titelman, performed
by Randy Newman; 'Memo
from Turner' by Mick
Jagger, Keith Richards,
performed by Mick Jagger
Sound Editor
Alan Pattillo
Sound Recording
Ron Barron
**Dialogue
Coach/Technical Adviser**
David Litvinoff

James Fox
Chas Devlin
Mick Jagger
Turner
Anita Pallenberg
Pherber
Michèle Breton
Lucy
Ann Sidney
Dana
John Bindon
Moody
Stanley Meadows
Rosebloom
Allan Cuthbertson
the lawyer
Antony Morton
Dennis
Johnny Shannon
Harry Flowers
Anthony Valentine
Joey Maddocks
Ken Colley
Tony Farrell
John Sterland
the chauffeur
Laraine Wickens
Lorraine

Colour by
Technicolor

9,180 feet
102 minutes

*Credits compiled by
Markku Salmi.*

BIBLIOGRAPHY

. . . .

Aftel, Mandy, *Death of a Rolling Stone: The Brian Jones Story* (London: Sidgwick & Jackson, 1982).

Ali, Tariq, *Street Fighting Years: An Autobiography of the 60s* (London: Collins, 1987).

Annan, Noel, *Our Age* (London: Weidenfeld & Nicolson, 1990).

Artaud, Antonin, *The Theatre and its Double*, Victor Corti (trs.) (London: Calder & Boyars, 1970).

Austin, J.L., *How to Do Things with Words* (Oxford: Clarendon Press, 1975).

Bataille, Georges, *L'eroticisme* (Paris: Editions de Minuit, 1957).

——— 'The Jesuve' and 'The Pineal Eye', in Allan Stoekl (ed.), *Visions of Excess* (Minnesota: University of Minnesota Press, 1985).

Berridge, Virginia, 'The Origins of the English Drug "Scene"', *Medical History*, vol. 32, 1988, pp. 51–64.

Borges, Jorge Luis, *Fictions*, Anthony Kerrigan, ed. (London: J. Calder, 1985).

Brown, Mick, 'Lights, Camera, Decadence', *Telegraph* Magazine, 3 June 1995.

Burroughs, William, *The Job: Interviews with Daniel Odier*. Revised edition with new Introduction 'Playback from Eden to Watergate' and 'Electronic Revolution' (New York: Grove Press, 1974).

Butler, Judith, *Gender Trouble: Feminism and the Subversion of Identity* (New York and London: Routledge, 1990).

——— *Bodies That Matter: On the Discursive Limits of 'Sex'* (New York and London: Routledge, 1993).

Carr, Gordon, *The Angry Brigade* (London: Gollancz, 1975).

Caute, David, *Sixty Eight: The Year of the Barricades* (London: Hamish Hamilton, 1988).

Charters, Ann (ed.), *The Penguin Book of the Beats* (London: Penguin, 1992).

Cohn, Nik, *Today There Are No Gentlemen* (London: Weidenfeld & Nicolson, 1971).

Connolly, Ray (ed.), *In the 60s* (London: Pavilion, 1995).

Cooper, David (ed.), *The Dialectics of Liberation* (London: Penguin, 1967).

Debord, Guy, *Society of the Spectacle* (New York: Zone Books, 1994).

Derrida, Jacques, 'Signature evenement contexte', in *La Dissemination* (Paris: Editions du Seuil, 1972), pp. 157–83.

——— 'Limited Inc. abc', *Glyph*, vol. 2, 1977, pp. 162–254.

Fabian, Jenny and Johnny Byrne, *Groupie* (London: Omnibus Press, 1997).

Faithfull, Marianne, *Faithfull* (London: Michael Joseph, 1994).

Fountain, Nigel, *Underground* (London: Pluto Press, 1988).

Fraser, Ronald, *1968: A Student Generation in Revolt* (London: Chatto & Windus, 1988).

Freud, Sigmund, 'Fetishism', in *The Complete Psychological Works of Sigmund Freud* (London: The Hogarth Press, 1961), vol. 21, pp. 152–7.

Gilroy, Paul, *The Black Atlantic: Modernity and Double Consciousness* (Cambridge, MA: Harvard University Press, 1993).

Goodman, Arnold, *Tell Them I'm On My Way* (London: Chapmans, 1993).

Gould, Tony, *Inside Outsider: The Life and Times of Colin MacInnes* (London: Chatto & Windus, 1983).

Green, Jonathon, *Days in the Life* (London: Heinemann, 1988).

Green, Shirley, *Rachman* (London: Michael Joseph, 1979).

Greene, Sir Hugh Carleton, *The Third Floor Front: A View of Broadcasting in the 60s* (London: The Bodley Head, 1969).

Greer, Germaine, *The Female Eunuch* (London: MacGibbon & Kee, 1970).

Haynes, Jim, *Thanks for Coming* (London: Faber, 1984).

Hayter, Alethea, *Opium and the Romantic Imagination* (London: Faber, 1968).

Hewison, Robert, *Too Much* (London: Methuen, 1986).

Hill, Lee, 'Performance Pieces –The Wild Life and Art of Donald Cammell'. Unpublished.

Home, Stuart (ed.), *What is Situationism? A Reader* (Edinburgh: AK Press, 1996).

Hughes, William, *Performance* (London: Tandem, 1970).

Jackson, Kevin, 'A Final Memo from Turner', *Guardian*, 9 May 1996.

Jameson, Fredric, *The Political Unconscious* (Ithaca: Cornell University Press, 1981).

Jeffrey-Poulter, Stephen, *Peers, Queers and Commons: The Struggle for Gay Law Reform from 1950 to the Present* (London: Routledge, 1991).

Knabb, Ken (ed.), *Situationist International Anthology* (Berkeley: Bureau of Public Service, 1981).

Kohn, Marek, *Dope Girls* (London: Lawrence and Wishart, 1992).

Lacan, Jacques, *Le Seminaire XX: encore* (Paris: Editions du Seuil, 1975).

Leary, Timothy, *The Politics of Ecstasy* (London: Paladin, 1970).

Levin, Bernard, *The Pendulum Years* (London: Cape, 1970).

MacInnes, Colin, *Absolute Beginners* (London: MacGibbon & Kee, 1959).

——————— *England, Half-English* (London: MacGibbon & Kee, 1961).

Mailer, Norman, *Advertisements for Myself* (London: Andre Deutsch, 1961).

Maitland, Sarah (ed.), *Very Heaven: Looking Back at the 60s* (London: Virago, 1988).

Marcus, Greil, *Lipstick Traces: A Secret History of the Twentieth Century* (London: Secker and Warburg, 1989).

Marsh, Dave, *Before I Get Old: The Story of the Who* (London: Plexus, 1983).

Melly, George, *Revolt into Style* (London: Penguin, 1970).

Miles, Barry, *McCartney* (London: Secker and Warburg, 1997).

Miller, Gavin, review of *Performance*, *The Listener*, 14 January 1971.

Milne, Tom, review of *Performance*, *Observer*, 9 January 1971.

Monthly Film Bulletin, vol. 38 no. 445, February 1971.

Murphy, Robert, *60s British Cinema* (London: BFI, 1992).

Neville, Richard, *Play Power* (London: Jonathan Cape, 1970).

——————— *Hippie Hippie Shake* (London: Bloomsbury, 1995).

Norman, Philip, *Shout: The True Story of the Beatles* (London: Elm Tree, 1981).

——————— *The Stones* (London: Elm Tree, 1984).

——————— *Everyone's Gone to the Moon* (London: Hutchinson, 1995).

Nuttal, Jeff, *Bomb Culture* (London: MacGibbon & Kee, 1968).

Obst, Linda Rosen (ed.), *The 60s* (London: Rolling Stone Press, 1977).

Parker, Andrew and Eve Kosofsky Sedgwick (eds), *Performativity and Performance* (New York and London: Routledge, 1995).

Pavis, Patrice (ed.), *The Intercultural Performance Reader* (London and New York: Routledge, 1996).

Pearson, John, *The Profession of Violence: The Rise and Fall of the Kray Twins* (London: Weidenfeld and Nicolson, 1972).

Phelan, Peggy, *The Politics of Performance* (London and New York: Routledge, 1993).

Pimlott, Ben, *Harold Wilson* (London: HarperCollins, 1992).

Richardson, Perry (ed.), *The Early Stones: Legendary Photographs of a Band in the Making 1963–73* (London: Secker and Warburg, 1995).

Rodley, Chris, 'Marlon Madness and Me', *20/20*, April 1989, pp. 38–51.

Roszak, Theodore M., *The Making of a Counter-Culture* (London: Faber, 1970).

Sanchez, Tony, *Up and Down with The Rolling Stones* (New York: Da Capo Press, 1996).

Savage, Jon, 'Tuning into Wonders: Interview with Christopher Gibbs', *Sight and Sound*, vol. 5. no. 9, pp. 24–5.

——————— 'Snapshots of the 60s', *Sight and Sound*, vol. 3. no. 5, May 1993, pp. 13–18.

Schickel, Richard, review of *Performance*, *Time*, 24 August 1970, p. 61.

Searle, John, *Speech Acts* (Cambridge: Cambridge University Press, 1969).

——————— 'Reiterating Differences', *Glyph*, vol. 1, 1977, pp. 198–208.

Simon, John, review of *Performance*, *New York Times*, 23 August 1970.

Sinclair, Iain, *Lights Out for the Territory* (London: Granta, 1997).

Singer, Daniel, *Prelude to Revolution: France in May, 1968* (London: Jonathan Cape, 1970).

Vague, Tom, *Anarchy in the UK: The Angry Brigade* (Edinburgh: AK Press, 1997).

Walker, Alexander, *Hollywood, England: The British Film Industry in the Sixties* (London: Michael Joseph, 1974).

Webb, James, *The Occult Establishment* (La Salle, IL: Open Court Books, 1976).

Weeks, Jeffrey, *Sex, Politics and Society* (London: Routledge, 1989). Second edition.

——— *Sexuality and its Discontents* (London: Routledge, 1985).

Williams, Raymond, *The Long Revolution* (London: Chatto & Windus, 1961).

Wilmut, Roger, *From Fringe to Flying Circus* (London: Methuen, 1980).

Wollen, Peter, 'Possession', *Sight and Sound*, vol. 5 no. 9, September 1995, pp. 20–3.

X, Michael, *From Michael de Freitas to Michael X* (London: Andre Deutsch, 1968).

ALSO PUBLISHED

If you would like further information about future BFI Film Classics or about other books on film, media and popular culture from BFI Publishing, please write to:

BFI Film Classics
BFI Publishing
21 Stephen Street
London W1P 2LN

BFI FILM
CLASSICS

BFI Film Classics '… could scarcely be improved upon … informative, intelligent, jargon-free companions.'
The Observer

Each book in the BFI Publishing Film Classics series honours a great film from the history of world cinema. With new titles published each year, the series is rapidly building into a collection representing some of the best writing on film. If you would like to receive further information about future Film Classics or about other books on film, media and popular culture from BFI Publishing, please fill in your name and address and return this card to the BFI.* (No stamp required if posted in the UK, Channel Islands, or Isle of Man.)

NAME _____

ADDRESS _____

_____

_____

POSTCODE _____

E-MAIL ADDRESS: _____

WHICH *BFI FILM CLASSIC* DID YOU BUY? _____

_____

* In North America and Asia (except India),
please return your card to:
University of California Press, Web Department,
2120 Berkeley Way, Berkeley, CA 94720, USA

**BFI Publishing
21 Stephen Street
FREEPOST 7
LONDON
W1E 4AN**